Deuteronomy &
2nd Corinthians

Read the Bible Again for the First Time

Echoes Bible

Volume V

2025

World English Bible (WEB)

Echoesbible.com

Deuteronomy & 2 Corinthians
Read the Bible Again for the First Time
Echoes Bible, Volume V, 2025

© 2025 Echoes Bible Foundation

The Echoes Bible Foundation is a non-profit Christian ministry dedicated to the discovery, dissemination, education and application of literary connections between the inspired books of the Bible. It is organized as a U.S. based 501(c)3.

Echoes Bible Foundation
13359 North Highway 183
Suite 406-679
Austin, Texas 78750
publish@echoesbible.org

Paul, the Apostle to the Gentiles, first acknowledged Jesus as the Messiah as a result of encountering him on the road to Damascus. Prior to that he had been known as Saul, a learned leader among the Pharisee sect of Judaism in 1st century Judea, a student of the revered rabbi Gamaliel. His thinking and imagination had been shaped by deep acquaintance with the Torah, Wisdom Literature, and Prophets (Tanakh), what Christians in the modern age generally call "the Old Testament." How, exactly, did his biblically shaped mind and soul guide his composition of his letters? The quotations from scripture are clear enough, but in ten years of study, we have discovered in the text echoes of the Old Testament structure, theme, and vocabulary in Paul's letters. In this volume, we will explore those echoes between the book of Deuteronomy and the Second Epistle to the Corinthians.

Dedication:
To Paul the Apostle

ISBN Paperback: 978-1-970720-02-0
Cover Design by Stephen Douglas Alexander, Layout by Echoes Bible Foundation

1. Christianity. 2. Bibles. 3. Bible Commentary. 4. Bible Study. 5. Old Testament. 6. New Testament.
I. Echoes Bible Foundation
II. Deuteronomy & 2 Corinthians. Read the Bible Again for the First Time. Echoes Bible. Volume V. 2025.

INTRODUCTION

Upon receiving the revelation from God on the road to Damascus, Paul's entire world was turned upside down. A zealous student of the Torah, having studied under Gamaliel (Acts 22:3), Paul would then spend about three years in Arabia and Damascus before going up to Jerusalem to meet Peter and James (Gal. 1:18–19). His time in Arabia must have included extended periods of revisiting the Torah, seeking to understand how he could have missed the work of Christ Jesus within it. How fascinating it would have been to sit beside Paul, to converse with him, as he began reading the Torah anew in the light of Christ. In Arabia, Paul would have started to perceive how Christ was inextricably present in every book, every story, every paragraph, and perhaps even every verse that he had studied so intently for so many years. Given God's call to him on the road to Damascus (Acts 26:17), Paul must also have re-read the Torah with an eye toward discerning God's plan to bring the Gentiles into a saving knowledge of Jesus Christ.

When Paul was set apart for ministry, he experienced the joy of sharing the Gospel directly with both Jew and Gentile. After establishing assemblies in various locations, he would then write letters to them. The New Testament preserves more than a dozen of these letters, now recognized as the inspired Word of God. Paul wrote in Greek, and when quoting the Old Testament, he necessarily did so in Greek as well, and his direct quotations are numerous. At times he also addressed topics by appealing to principle rather than direct quotation. With great conviction he affirms that "every Scripture is inspired by God and profitable for teaching, for reproof, for correction, and for training in righteousness" (2 Tim. 3:16). Yet Paul is not an easy writer to understand. Peter himself acknowledges this in 2 Peter 3:16, observing that Paul's writings contain elements that are difficult to grasp and therefore more susceptible to being twisted.

The document you hold in your hand is likely unlike any other Bible you have encountered. The Echoes Bible Foundation asserts that this approach to reading the Scriptures is more firmly grounded than ever, for it provides additional insight into how—and from where—Paul formulated his words, anchoring his approach directly back to the inspired Word of God itself. This work enables the reader to study the books of Deuteronomy and 2 Corinthians side by side, section by section, and to see firsthand from where part of Paul's inspiration was drawn.

Our claim is that Paul used the book of Deuteronomy, first, as his outline when addressing the church at Corinth. Deuteronomy is a story of the interaction of Moses with his people on the banks of the Jordan as they prepare to enter the Promised Land. Moses reminds them of God purposes for them along with correction and concern for their future. It also reveals the complex relationship Moses has with the people, and his trust that they are in good hands with Joshua's leadership. Paul's second letter to the Corinthians has similar purposes and reveals his complex relationship with the assembly in Corinth, and his trust that they are in good hands with Titus whom he has sent to them. Both books also include very personal accounts of God's interaction with both men: Moses and Paul.

The following table shows a sampling of some of the echoes in Deuteronomy and how they inspired some of Paul's verses.

Deuteronomy	2 Corinthians
1 Ten regions listed of God's Promised Land	1 Ten different facets of God's "comfort"
4 Don't add a word to what I command	3 You are a letter of Christ
4 Written on two stone tables	3 Not in tablets of stone but hearts of flesh
7 The covenant and the lovingkindness	4 We preach Christ Jesus as Lord
9 Then I stayed on the Mountain 40 days/nights	5 A house not made with hands, eternal in heavens
10 Love the foreigner for you were such in Egypt	5 Christ gave to us the ministry of reconciliation
14 Rules for eating kosher	7 Let us cleanse ourselves from all defilement
18 Moses: God will raise up among you a prophet like me	10 I Paul, myself, entreat you in the humility and gentleness of Christ
20 When battle a people more numerous than you	10 We aren't bold to number or compare ourselves
21 Captive? Let her go because you humbled her	11 Did I commit a sin in humbling myself for you?
27 The 12 curses on Mt. Ebal recited	11 Paul lists 12 instances of suffering for Christ
29 A root that produces bitter poison	12 Paul reveals his "thorn in the flesh"
31 Moses commissions Joshua to lead in his place	12 Paul sends Titus to the Corinthians in his place
32 The song of Moses sung over the people	12 Paul may come mourn for unrepentant sinners

This document divides Deuteronomy and 2 Corinthians into 127 *sectional pairings*, each consisting of connections between one or more verses from the two books. Because Deuteronomy contains more verses than 2 Corinthians, a greater number of verses from Deuteronomy are, on average, paired with fewer verses from 2 Corinthians. These **pairings** are presented in a side-by-side format so that the reader may discern what in Deuteronomy may have partially inspired Paul in writing his corresponding words to the 2 Corinthians. Within each **pairing**, we have also identified what we believe to be more specific connections between particular statements in Deuteronomy and the words of Paul. We refer to these more specific, individual connections as *echoes*, and in this document we have identified almost 500 echoes.

For example, in Deuteronomy 1:1, the word "**Moses**" at the beginning of the verse is paired with the word "**Paul**" 2 Corinthians 1:1. This constitutes the first echo. Next, the phrase "**by the way**" is paired with the phrase "**through the will**" in 2 Corinthians 1:1. This constitutes the second echo, drawing a parallel between Aaron, the brother of Moses, and Sosthenes, the brother in Christ. The use of **bold underline** does not suggest that the second echo carries greater importance than the first; it functions solely as a visual aid to allow the reader's eye to identify corresponding echoes quickly. At times, non-bold underlining is also used.

In this initial sectional pairing, a total of five echoes are identified. Of particular note, in the fourth echo, the word Moab, is a form of "ab" or "av" meaning father. These five identified echoes may not be the only echoes present; however, in a black-and-white print format we have intentionally restricted our selection to those echoes that appear in sequential order.

For example, in a sectional pairing containing eight echoes, the first bolded echo in Deuteronomy will always and only be paired with the first bolded phrase in 2 Corinthians, and so forth through the section. Moreover, while Paul generally followed the sequence of Deuteronomy in his letter, nothing prevented him from summarizing a section of Deuteronomy with a single statement (see 2 Cor. 12:21). Notes appear after many pairings to explain less obvious echoes and any exceptions in format.

The *Echoes Bible* employs the World English Bible (WEB) translation, as it is available without copyright restrictions. At the same time, we often select echoes with careful attention to the Hebrew and Greek underlying the English words, and we frequently highlight such insights in the notes. That being said, the reader is encouraged to view the identified echoes as suggested connections between two inspired texts. While our suggestions themselves are not necessarily inspired, we firmly believe that the sheer preponderance, the richness of meaning, and the poetic beauty of these echoes will, in their totality, deepen a reader's love for God's Word, heighten their awe of God, and perhaps even carry them back to the joy of their first encounter with salvation—allowing them to *read the Bible again for the first time.*

The connections between these two books are real and we believe, intentional. The inspired text of Deuteronomy, helping to awaken Paul's vast knowledge of scripture in many other passages, overshadowed by the living work of the Holy Spirit, has resulted in the God-breathed inspired words of 2 Corinthians that we read today. Because the Word of God is inspired, we have every expectation that the Holy Spirit can speak to the reader through the Echoes Bible and reveal the truth of God's intentions in the words written by Paul.

Our vision is not that any new truth would emerge from these pairings, but rather that the echoes would further demonstrate how Paul's words are firmly anchored in the truth of all Scripture, thereby greatly reducing the potential for errors in interpretation. In agreement with Peter's warning, we likewise desire that Paul's words will no longer be twisted by "ignorant or unsettled persons."

The Echoes Bible Editing Team

Deuteronomy 1	2 Corinthians 1

De 1:1 These are the words which **Moses** spoke to all Israel beyond the Jordan in the wilderness, in the Arabah near Suph, between Paran, Tophel, Laban, Hazeroth, and Dizahab. **2** It is eleven days' journey from Horeb **by the way** of Mount Seir to Kadesh Barnea. **3** In the fortieth year, in the eleventh month, on the first day of the month, Moses spoke to **the children of Israel** according to all that Yahweh had given him in commandment to them, **4** after he had struck Sihon the king of the Amorites who lived in Heshbon, and Og the king of Bashan who lived in Ashtaroth, at Edrei. **5** Beyond the Jordan, in the land of **Moab**, Moses began to **declare this law**, saying,

2Cor 1:1 **Paul**, an apostle of Christ Jesus **through the will** of God, and Timothy our brother, to the assembly of God which is at Corinth, **with all the saints** who are in the whole of Achaia:

2 Grace to you and peace from God our **Father** and the **Lord Jesus Christ**.

NOTE: [Devarim.] In Deuteronomy 1:5, "Moab" in Hebrew means "from my father," echoing "Father." In the same verse, "law" is *torah* in Hebrew and so "declare this law" echoes the ministry of Jesus Christ who is the living word who became flesh and dwelt among us (John 1:1,14) and in this ministry "fulfilled the law" (Matthew 5:17).

NOTE: Devarim (Hebrew name for Deuteronomy) is divided into eleven Jewish Torah portions (Parshat), the first matching the book's name. The Echoes Bible's sections align with these boundaries and are marked with brackets in the notes.

De 1:6 "Yahweh our God spoke to us in Horeb, saying, 'You have lived long enough at this mountain. **7 Turn, and take your journey,** and go to the hill country of the Amorites and to all the places near there: in the Arabah, in the hill country, in the lowland, in the South, by the seashore, the land of the Canaanites, and Lebanon, as far as the great river, the river Euphrates. 8 Behold, I have set the land before you. Go in and possess the land which Yahweh swore to your fathers—to Abraham, to Isaac, and to Jacob—to give to them and to their offspring after them.'

9 I spoke to you at that time, saying, 'I am not able to bear you myself alone.

2Cor 1:3 Blessed be the God and Father of our Lord Jesus Christ, the Father of **mercies** and God of all comfort, **4** who comforts us in all our affliction, that we may be able to comfort those who are in any affliction, through the comfort with which we ourselves are comforted by God. **5** For as the sufferings of Christ abound to us, even so our comfort also abounds through Christ. **6** But if we are afflicted, it is for your comfort and salvation. If we are comforted, it is for your comfort, which produces in you the patient enduring of the same sufferings which we also suffer. **7** Our hope for you is steadfast, knowing that, since you are partakers of the sufferings, so you are also of the comfort.

NOTE: Concerning the proposed echo between "turn, and take your journey" and "mercies," God's decision to bring the children of Israel into the promised land was not a reward for their good behavior! The Father of mercies gives to us first, and desires that we respond in kind. Paul, in 2 Corinthians 1:3-7 writes the word "comfort" ten times, which echoes in Deuteronomy 1:7, the ten regions of the promised land that God gave his people. Moses admits in verse Deut. 1:9 that he is not able to bear these things on his own, implying that God's comfort is needed. The process of possessing the land was very difficult with many afflictions and sufferings, but the actual possession of it brings immediate comfort. Thus God through Christ is shown to be both the Father of *mercies*, and the God of all *comfort*.

De 1:10 Yahweh your God has **multiplied** you, and behold, you are today as the stars of the sky for multitude. **11** May Yahweh, the God of your fathers, make you a thousand times as many as you are and bless you, as he has promised you! **12** How can **I myself alone bear** your problems, your burdens, and your strife?

2Cor 1:5 For as the sufferings of Christ abound to us, even so our comfort also **abounds** through Christ. **6** But if we are afflicted, it is for your comfort and salvation. If we are comforted, it is for your comfort, which produces in you the patient enduring of the same sufferings which **we also suffer**. **7** Our hope for you is steadfast, knowing that, since you are partakers of the sufferings, so you are also of the comfort.

NOTE: In Deuteronomy 1:12, Moses describes three sufferings he bears from the people. In 2 Corinthians 1:5-7 Paul lists *sufferings* three times, but frames it towards the mutually shared sufferings between his ministry team, and the church. In other words, while Moses said he must bear these alone, Paul speaks of a mutual sharing of sufferings, bringing the church into the same sufferings as Paul and his team. Besides 2 Cor. 1:5, Paul writes about the "fellowship of his sufferings" in Philippians 3:10. No truth "seen" in the Echoes Bible should ever stand alone, it must always find its confirmation directly in unrelated passages.

De 1:13 Take wise **men of understanding** who are respected among your tribes, and I will make them heads over you. **14** You answered me, and said, "The thing which you have spoken is good to do." **15** So I took the heads of your tribes, wise and respected men, and made them heads over you, captains of thousands, captains of hundreds, captains of fifties, captains of tens, and officers, according to your tribes.

16 I commanded your judges at that time, saying, "Hear cases between your brothers and judge righteously between a man and his brother, and the foreigner who is living with him. **17** You shall not show **partiality in judgment**; you shall hear **the small** and the great alike. You shall not be afraid of the face of man, for the judgment is God's. **The case that is too hard for you, you shall bring to me**, and I will hear it." **18** I commanded you at that time all the things which you should do.

2Cor 1:8 For we **don't desire to have you uninformed, brothers**, concerning our affliction which happened to us in Asia, that we were **weighed down** exceedingly, **beyond our power**, so much that we despaired even of life. **9** Yes, we ourselves have had the sentence of death within ourselves, **that we should not trust in ourselves, but in God who raises the dead**,

NOTE: In 2 Corinthians 1:8, the phrase "weighed down" echoes in Deuteronomy the idea of what *should be* balanced scales in judgment, but that instead have been altered, (i.e. weighed against them through partiality). Unfair judgement is easier to achieve against the "small" rather than the great, which Paul echoes in the phrase "beyond our power," meaning they had no leverage to change the situation into their own favor. The statement in Deut. 1:17, "the case that is too hard for you, you shall bring to me" is a statement Paul makes towards God directly, rather than appealing to any human judge, because Paul has no human being, no "Moses" towards whom to make his appeal.

De 1:19 We traveled from Horeb and went **through all that great and terrible wilderness** which you saw, by the way to the hill country of the Amorites, as Yahweh our God commanded us; and we came to Kadesh Barnea. **20** I said to you, "You have come to the hill country of the Amorites, which Yahweh our God gives to us. **21** <u>Behold, Yahweh your God has set the land before you</u>. Go up, take possession, as Yahweh the God of your fathers has spoken to you. Don't be afraid, neither be dismayed."

22 You came near to me, every one of you, and said, "Let's send men before us, that they may search the land for us, and bring back to us word by what way we must go up, **and the cities to which we shall come**." **23** The thing pleased me well. I took twelve of your men, one man for every tribe. **24 They turned and went up into the hill country, and came to the valley of Eshcol, and spied it out**. **25** They took some of the <u>fruit of the land in their hands and brought it down to us</u>, and brought us word again, and said, "It is a good land which Yahweh our God gives to us.

2Cor 1:10 who **delivered us out of so great a death**, and does deliver, on <u>whom we have set our hope that he will also still deliver us</u>, **11** you **also helping together on our behalf by your supplication**; that, <u>for the gift given to us by means of many</u>, thanks may be given by many persons on your behalf. **12** For our boasting is this: the testimony of our conscience that in holiness and sincerity of God, not in fleshly wisdom but in the grace of God, we **behaved ourselves in the world**, and <u>more abundantly toward you</u>.

NOTE: In Deuteronomy 1:22, when all people came and said to Moses, "Let's send men before us" to bring back word about "the cities to which we shall come," by their faith in the coming victory, the people were actually aiding Moses with his supplication that God's command to take the land would be realized! According to the Paul's echo, speaking according to principle, had the cities of Canaan actually been taken as God commanded, thanks for the gift (of the cities) should be given to all the people for their initial supplication to Moses in Deut. 1:22, not just those twelve who spied it out in Deut. 1:24. In the same way Paul is enlarging the thinking of the Corinthians to see themselves as helping God's work in Christ through their supplication alongside Pauls' team.

De 1:26 Yet you wouldn't go up, but rebelled against the commandment of Yahweh your God. **27** You murmured in your tents, and said, "Because Yahweh hated us, he has brought us out of the land of Egypt, to deliver us into the hand of the Amorites to destroy us. **28 Where are we going up? Our brothers have made our heart melt**, saying, 'The people are greater and taller than we. The cities are great and fortified up to the sky. Moreover we have seen the sons of the Anakim there!'" **29** Then I said to you, "Don't be terrified. **Don't be afraid of them. 30 Yahweh your God, who goes before you, he will fight for you**, according to all that he did for you in Egypt before your eyes, **31** and in the wilderness where you have seen how that Yahweh your God carried you, as a man carries his son, in all the way that you went, until you came to this place." **32** Yet in this thing you didn't believe Yahweh your God, **33** who went before you on the way, to seek out a place for you to pitch your tents in: in fire by night, to show you by what way you should go, and in the cloud by **day**.

2Cor 1:13 For we write no other things to you than what you read or even acknowledge, and I hope you will **acknowledge** to the end— **14** as also you **acknowledged** us in part—that we are your boasting, even as you also are ours, in the **day** of our Lord Jesus.

NOTE: In 2 Corinthians, "acknowledge" can be translated "understand." In this passage, of Deuteronomy, the people express three statements of no understanding in Deuteronomy 1: 27-28: "Because Yahweh hated us, he has brought us out," "Where are we going up" (also translated "Can we go up?"), and "Our brothers have made our heart melt." In return Moses speaks three statements of understanding in Deut. 1:29-30: "Don't be terrified," "Don't be afraid." "Yahweh…will fight for you."

De 1:34 Yahweh heard the voice of your words and was angry, and swore, saying, **35** "Surely not one of these men of this evil generation shall see the good land which I swore to give to your fathers, **36 except Caleb the son of Jephunneh.** He shall see it. To him I will give the land that he has trodden on, and to his children, because he has wholly followed Yahweh." **37** Also Yahweh was angry with me for your sakes, saying, "You also shall not go in there. **38** Joshua the son of Nun, who stands before you, **shall go in there**. Encourage him, for he shall cause Israel to inherit it. 39 Moreover your little ones, whom you said would be captured or killed, your children, who today have no knowledge of good or evil, <u>they shall go in there. To them I will give it, and they shall possess it</u>. **40 But as for you, turn, and take your journey into the wilderness by the way to the Red Sea**."

41 Then you answered and said to me, "We have sinned against Yahweh. **We will go up and fight**, <u>according to all that Yahweh our God commanded us.</u>" Every man of you put on his weapons of war, and presumed to go up into the hill country. **42** Yahweh said to me, "Tell them, '**Don't go up and don't fight**; for I am not among you, lest you be struck before your enemies.'" **43** So I spoke to you, and you didn't listen; but you rebelled against the commandment of Yahweh, and were presumptuous, and went up into the hill country. **44** The Amorites, who lived in that hill country, came out against you and chased you as bees do, and beat you down in Seir, even to Hormah. **45 You returned and wept before Yahweh, but Yahweh didn't listen to your voice, nor turn his ear to you**.

2Cor 1:15 In this confidence, I was determined **to come first to you**, that you might have a second benefit, **16** and by you to **pass into Macedonia**, and again from Macedonia to come to you, and to be <u>sent forward by you on my journey to Judea</u>. **17 When I therefore planned this, did I show fickleness**? Or the things that I plan, **do I plan according to the flesh**, that with me there should be the "Yes, yes" and the "No, no?" **18** But as God is faithful, **our word toward you was not "Yes and no."**

NOTE: The first plan was for Paul to come to Corinth, and for Moses and Caleb to enter to the promised land (echo 1). That plan changed somewhat for Paul, and it changed for Moses when God decided Joshua would go in his place (echo 2), and the young children will go in later (echo 3). And when God said take your journey in the wilderness, was God showing fickleness (echo 4)? And then when the people realized they had sinned, and wanted now to fight, was it not by the flesh (echo 5)? And were they not justifying their fleshly decision by taking God's previous "yes" as their present "yes" (echo 6)? But when seeing their hearts were not right, and God said to them, "Don't go up and fight," was that not God contradicting his own "yes" with a "no" (echo 7)? And when, after they failed in the attempt, the people wept before Yahweh, and He would no longer answer them with a "yes" or "no" but had to remain silent, had God just proven he was rejecting them entirely (echo 8)? For the answer see the note in the next sectional pairing.

De 1:46 So you **stayed in Kadesh many days**, according to the days that **you remained**.	**2Cor 1:19** For the Son of God, Jesus Christ, who was preached among you by us—by me, Silvanus, and Timothy—was not "Yes and no," but in him is "Yes." **20 For however many are the promises of God, in him is the "Yes." Therefore also through him is the "Amen," to the glory of God through us**. 21 Now he who **establishes us** with you in Christ and anointed us is God, 22 who also sealed us and gave us the down payment of the Spirit in our hearts.

NOTE: God had not rejected his people! While the original "yes" was still a "yes," God's "yes" now had to be delivered in a very different way over a much longer period of time. The best way for God to communicate that "yes" was for the cloud and fire to remain in view, (showing God's faithfulness) but for them not to move anywhere immediately, but to stay many days in Kadesh, which appropriately means "sacred." Nevertheless that stay in Kadesh must have been a time of great sorrow and mourning.

Deuteronomy 2   2 Cor. 1:23

De 2:1 Then we turned, and took our journey into the wilderness by the way to the Red Sea, as Yahweh spoke to me; and **we encircled Mount Seir many days**. 2 Yahweh spoke to me, saying, 3 'You have encircled this mountain long enough. Turn northward. 4 Command the people, saying, "You are to pass through the border of your brothers, the children of Esau, who dwell in Seir; and they will be afraid of you. Therefore be careful. 5 **Don't contend with them**; for I will not give you any of their land, no, not so much as for the sole of the foot to tread on, because **I have given Mount Seir to Esau for a possession**. 6 You shall purchase food from them for money, that you may eat. You shall also buy water from them for money, that you may drink." 7 For Yahweh your God has blessed you in all the work of your hand. He has known your walking through this great wilderness. These forty years, **Yahweh your God has been with you**. You have lacked nothing.'	**2Cor 1:23** But I call God for a witness to my soul, **that I didn't come to Corinth** to **spare you**. 24 We don't control your faith but **are fellow workers with you** for your joy. For **you stand firm in faith**.

NOTE: Although God had told Israel not to pass through the region of Esau, it wasn't as though God was saying Esau didn't deserve correction. Thus "don't contend with them" echoes "spare you." Nevertheless, Israel was not given control over the children of Esau and their land, and neither was Paul given control over the way the Corinthians would exercise their faith. Thus, "I have given Mount Seir to Esau for a possession" echoes "are fellow workers with you.

Deuteronomy 2:8	2 Corinthians 2

De 2:8 So we passed by from our brothers, the children of Esau, who dwell in Seir, from the way of the Arabah, from Elath and from Ezion Geber. We turned and passed by the way of the wilderness of Moab. **9** Yahweh said to me, "Don't bother Moab, neither contend with them in battle; for I will not give you any of his land for a possession, because I have given Ar to the children of Lot for a possession." **10** (The Emim lived there before, a great and numerous people, and tall as the Anakim. **11** They were accounted Rephaim, as the Anakim; but the Moabites call them Emim. **12** The Horites also lived in Seir before, but the children of Esau succeeded them. They destroyed them from before them, and lived in their place, as Israel did to the land of his possession, which Yahweh gave to them.) **13** 'Now rise up and cross over the brook Zered.' We went over the brook Zered. **14** <u>The days in which we came from Kadesh Barnea</u> until we had come over the brook Zered were thirty-eight years, **until all the generation of the men of war were consumed from the middle of the camp, as Yahweh swore to them**.

2**Cor 2:1** But I determined this for myself, that **I would not come to you again in sorrow**. **2** For if I make you sorry, then who will make me glad but he who is made sorry by me? **3** And I wrote this very thing to you, so that when I came, I wouldn't have sorrow from them of whom I ought to rejoice; having confidence in you all that my joy would be shared by all of you. **4** For out of much **<u>affliction and anguish of heart</u> I wrote to you with many tears, not that you should be made sorry, but that you might know the love that I have so abundantly for you**.

NOTE: See Deuteronomy 1:46 regarding the echo of "Kadesh" with "anguish of heart."

De 2:15 <u>Moreover Yahweh's hand was against them, to destroy them from the middle of the camp</u>, until they were consumed.

16 So when all the men of war were consumed and dead from among the people, **17** Yahweh spoke to me, saying, **18** 'You are to pass over Ar, the border of Moab, today. **19** When you come near the border of the children of Ammon, don't bother them, nor contend with them; for I will not give you any of the land of the children of Ammon for a possession, because I have given it to the children of Lot for a possession.' **20** (That also is considered a land of Rephaim. Rephaim lived there before, but the Ammonites call them Zamzummim, **21** a great people, many, and tall, as the Anakim; but Yahweh destroyed them from before them, and they succeeded them, and lived in their place; **22** as he did for the children of Esau who dwell in Seir, when he destroyed the Horites from before them; and they succeeded them, and lived in their place even to this day. **23** Then the Avvim, who lived in villages as far as Gaza: the Caphtorim, who came out of Caphtor, destroyed them and lived in their place.) **24** 'Rise up, take your journey, and pass over the valley of the Arnon. **Behold, I have given into your hand Sihon the Amorite, king of Heshbon, and his land; begin to possess it, and contend with him in battle**. **25** Today I will begin to put the dread of you and the fear of you on the peoples who are under the whole sky, who shall hear the report of you, and shall tremble and be in anguish because of you.'

2Cor 2:5 <u>But if any has caused sorrow, he has caused sorrow, not to me, but in part (that I not press too heavily) to you all</u>.

6 This punishment which was inflicted by the many is sufficient for such a one; **7** so that on the contrary you should rather forgive him and comfort him, lest by any means such a one should be swallowed up with his excessive sorrow. **8** Therefore I beg you to confirm your love toward him. **9** For to this end I also wrote, that I might know the proof of you, whether you are obedient in all things. **10** Now I also forgive whomever you forgive anything. For if indeed I have forgiven anything, I have forgiven that one for your sakes in the presence of Christ, **11 that no advantage may be gained over us by Satan, for we are not ignorant of his schemes**.

NOTE: Here, Sihon the Amorite is echoing the work of Satan in the mind of Paul.

De 2:26 I sent messengers out of the wilderness of Kedemoth to Sihon king of **Heshbon** with <u>words of peace</u>, saying, **27** "**Let me pass through your land**. I will go along by the highway. I will turn neither to the right hand nor to the left. **28** You shall sell me food for money, that I may eat; and give me water for money, that I may drink. Just let me pass through on my feet, **29** as the children of Esau who dwell in Seir, and the Moabites who dwell in Ar, did to me, until I pass over the Jordan into the land which Yahweh our God gives us." **30** But Sihon king of Heshbon would not let us pass by him, for Yahweh your **God hardened his spirit** and made his heart obstinate, that he might deliver him into your hand, as it is today. **31** Yahweh said to me, "Behold, I have begun to deliver up Sihon and his land before you. Begin to possess, that you may inherit his land."

2Cor 2:12 Now when I came to **Troas** for the **Good News of Christ**, and when a **door was opened** to me in the Lord, **13** I had **no relief for my spirit**, because I didn't find Titus, my brother, but taking my leave of them, I went out into Macedonia.

NOTE: The word Heshbon means "stronghold." Troas meaning "plain of Troy" was a stronghold that the Greeks attempted to conquer for about ten years, finally succeeding through the famous "Trojan horse" ruse. While Moses offered Sihon of Heshbon words of peace, and Paul brought the good news of Christ to Troas, neither city was able to fully accept the words that were being offered in good faith.

De 2:32 Then Sihon came out against us, he and all his people, to battle at Jahaz. **33** Yahweh our **God delivered him up before us**; and we struck him, his sons, and all his people. **34** We took all his cities at that time, and <u>utterly destroyed every inhabited city, with the women and the little ones. We left no one remaining</u>. **35** Only the livestock we took for plunder for ourselves, with the spoil of the cities which we had taken. **36** From Aroer, which is on the edge of the valley of the Arnon, and the city that is in the valley, even to Gilead, **there was not a city too high for us. Yahweh our God delivered up all before us**. **37** Only to the land of the children of Ammon you didn't come near: all the banks of the river Jabbok, and the cities of the hill country, and wherever Yahweh our God forbade us.

2Cor 2:14 Now thanks be to **God who always leads us** in <u>triumph in Christ</u>, and **reveals through us the sweet aroma of his knowledge in every place**.

NOTE: Paul never echoes the conquest of Israel with the destruction of persons, only the destruction of evil! Here we see that in Paul's mind to triumph in Christ is to bring a sweet aroma of the knowledge of Christ to that very location. Ultimately God gave the Promised Land to Israel so that his ways could be known to the world. As long as the people Heshbon were worshipping false gods, those places could never experience the sweet aroma of God's presence. This theme continues in the next pairing. See also the notes after Deuteronomy 7:12 and 18:9.

Deuteronomy 3   2 Cor. 2:15

De 3:1 Then we turned, and went up the way to Bashan. Og the king of Bashan came out against us, he and all his people, to battle at Edrei. **2** Yahweh said to me, "Don't fear him; **for I have delivered him, with all his people and his land, into your hand**. You shall do to him as you did to Sihon king of the Amorites, who lived at Heshbon." **3** So Yahweh our God also delivered into our hand Og, the king of Bashan, and all his people. We struck him until no one was left to him remaining. **4** We took all his cities at that time. There was not a city which we didn't take from them: sixty cities, all the region of Argob, the kingdom of Og in Bashan. **5** All these were cities fortified with high walls, gates, and bars, in addition to a great many villages without walls. **6** We utterly destroyed them, as we did to Sihon king of Heshbon, utterly destroying every inhabited city, with the women and the little ones. **7** But all the livestock, and the spoil of the cities, we took for plunder for ourselves.

8 We took the land at that time out of the hand of the two kings of the Amorites who were beyond the Jordan, from the valley of the Arnon to Mount Hermon. **9** (The Sidonians call Hermon Sirion, and the Amorites call it Senir.) **10** We took all the cities of the plain, and all Gilead, and all Bashan, to Salecah and Edrei, cities of the kingdom of Og in Bashan. **11** (For only Og king of Bashan remained of the remnant of the Rephaim. Behold, his bedstead was a bedstead of iron. Isn't it in Rabbah of the children of Ammon? Nine cubits was its length, and four cubits its width, after the cubit of a man.)

12 **This land we took in possession at that time**: from Aroer, which is by the valley of the Arnon, and half the hill country of Gilead with its cities, I gave to the Reubenites and to the Gadites; **13** and the rest of Gilead, and all Bashan, the kingdom of Og, I gave to the half-tribe of Manasseh—all the region of Argob, even all Bashan. (The same is called the land of Rephaim. **14** Jair the son of Manasseh took all the region of Argob, to the border of the Geshurites and the Maacathites, and called them, even Bashan, after his own name, Havvoth Jair, to this day.) **15** I gave Gilead to Machir. **16** To the Reubenites and to the Gadites I gave from Gilead even to the valley of the Arnon, the middle of the valley, and its border, even to the river Jabbok, which is the border of the children of Ammon; **17** the Arabah also, and the Jordan and its border, from Chinnereth even to the sea of the Arabah, the Salt Sea, under the slopes of Pisgah eastward.

2**Cor 2:15** For we are a sweet **aroma of Christ to God in those who are saved and in those who perish**: **16** to the one a stench from death to death, to the other a sweet aroma **from life to life**. Who is sufficient for these things?

NOTE: See note in the previous pairing.

De 3:18 I commanded you at that time, saying, **'Yahweh your God has given you this land to possess it**. All the men of valor shall pass over armed before your brothers, the children of Israel. **19** But your wives, and your little ones, and your livestock (I know that you have much livestock), shall stay in your cities which I have given you, **20** until Yahweh gives rest to your brothers, as to you, and they also <u>possess the land which Yahweh your God gives them</u> beyond the Jordan. Then you shall each return to his own possession, which I have given you.' **21** I commanded Joshua at that time, saying, **'Your eyes have seen all that Yahweh your God has done** to these two kings. So shall Yahweh do to all the kingdoms where you <u>go over</u>. **22** <u>You shall not fear them; for Yahweh your God himself fights for you</u>."

2Cor 2:17 For we are not as so many, peddling the word of God. **But as of sincerity**, but <u>as of God</u>, in the **sight of God**, <u>we speak in Christ</u>.

NOTE: [Devarim ends.] Concerning the first echo, the purpose of crossing the Jordan was not primarily to defeat the enemies of Israel, but to possess the land, meaning to live there, improve it, and make it a home. Their relocation was not a means to some other end. In this way "possessing" the land echoes "sincerity." In Deuteronomy 3:21, "Go over," *abar* in Hebrew, means to pass over. Since Christ is our "Passover," when we "pass over" we do so in Christ.

Deuteronomy 3:23   2 Cor. 3

De 3:23 I begged Yahweh at that time, saying, **24** "O Lord Yahweh, you have begun to show your servant your greatness, and your strong hand. For what god is there in heaven or in earth that can do works like yours, and according to your mighty acts? **25** Please let me go over and see the good land that is beyond the Jordan, that fine mountain, and Lebanon." **26** But Yahweh was angry with me for your sakes, and didn't listen to me. He said to me, "Let it suffice you. Speak no more to me of this matter. **27** Go up to the top of Pisgah, and lift up your eyes westward, and northward, and southward, and eastward, and see with your eyes; for you shall not go over this Jordan. **28** But **commission Joshua**, and encourage him, and strengthen him; for he shall go over before this people, and **he shall cause them to inherit the land which you shall see**." **29** So we stayed in the valley near Beth Peor.

2Cor 3:1 **Are we beginning again to commend ourselves**? Or do we need, as do some, letters of commendation to you or from you? **2 You are our letter, written in our hearts**, known and read by all men.

NOTE: [Va'etchanan.] In the first echo, Moses wanted to go in himself, but he could not. So he commissioned Joshua to do in action what he could not do. Then why would Paul say to the Corinthians, "you are our letter?" The word letter in Greek literally means "to bridle or stop up the mouth," and/or "to reduce to silence." This is exactly what God said to Moses in Deut.3:26, saying "Speak no more to me of this matter." In the second echo, Moses would not join them to inherit the land, but that which Moses had written to them, would through them, become known and read by all the world. Yet, without inheritance of the land, Israel's testimony to the world would have completely failed. In the same way, when the Corinthians reveal the sweet aroma of Christ in their regions of influence, when the Corinthians walk in sincerity, but as of God, in the sight of God, speak in Christ, they become the evidence to the world of that Good News Paul had hoped to preach everywhere.

Deuteronomy 4   ## 2 Cor. 3:3

De 4:1 Now, Israel, listen to the statutes and to the ordinances which I teach you, to do them; that you may live and go in and possess the land which Yahweh, the God of your fathers, gives you. **2** You shall not add to the **word which I command you, neither shall you take away from it, that you may keep the commandments of Yahweh your God** which I command you. **3** Your eyes have seen what Yahweh did because of Baal Peor; for all the men who followed Baal Peor, Yahweh your God has destroyed them from among you. **4** But you who were faithful to Yahweh your God are all alive today.

5 Behold, <u>I have taught you statutes and ordinances, even as Yahweh my God commanded me</u>, that you should do so in the middle of the land where you go in to possess it. **6** Keep therefore and do them; for this is your wisdom and your understanding in the sight of the peoples who shall hear all these statutes and say, "Surely this great nation is a wise and understanding people." **7** For what great nation is there that has a god so near to them as Yahweh our God is whenever we call on him? **8** What great nation is there that has statutes and ordinances so righteous as all this law which I set before you today?

2Cor 3:3a being revealed that **you are a letter of Christ**, <u>served by us</u>,

NOTE: This pairing continues to develop the theme of the prior pairing, continuing into the next pairing.

De 4:9 Only be careful, and keep your soul diligently, lest you forget the things which your eyes saw, and lest they depart from your heart all the days of your life; but make them known to your children and your children's children— **10** the day that you stood before Yahweh your God in Horeb, when Yahweh said to me, "Assemble the people to me, and I will make them hear my words, that they may learn to fear me all the days that they live on the earth, and that they may teach their children." **11** You came near and stood under the mountain. The mountain burned with fire to the heart of the sky, with darkness, cloud, and thick darkness. **12 Yahweh spoke to you out of the middle of the fire: you heard the voice of words, but you saw no form; only you heard a voice**. **13** He declared to you his covenant, which he commanded you to perform, even the ten commandments. He wrote them on two stone tablets. **14** Yahweh commanded me at that time to teach you statutes and ordinances, that you might do them in the land where you go over to possess it.

15 Be very careful, for you saw no kind of form on the day that Yahweh spoke to you in Horeb out of the middle of the fire, **16** lest you corrupt yourselves, and make yourself a carved image in the form of any figure, the likeness of male or female, **17** the likeness of any animal that is on the earth, the likeness of any winged bird that flies in the sky, **18** the likeness of anything that creeps on the ground, the likeness of any fish that is in the water under the earth; **19** and lest you lift up your eyes to the sky, and when you see the sun and the moon and the stars, even all the army of the sky, you are drawn away and worship them, and serve them, which Yahweh your God has allotted to all the peoples under the whole sky. **20 But Yahweh has taken you, and brought you out of the iron furnace, out of Egypt, to be to him a people of inheritance, as it is today**.

2Cor 3:3b written **not with ink, but with the Spirit of the living God**; not in tablets of stone, but in **tablets that are hearts of flesh**.

NOTE: Deuteronomy 4:12 references the Jewish tradition of the "Torah of fire" given at Mount Sinai. The third echo, Deuteronomy 4:20 as in Deut. 3:28 previously, the idea of a people of God's inheritance is linked with God's word that dwells in human hearts. God was not satisfied with commandments written in stone; he wanted a people who would have those commandments carried inside them. This is evidenced by the first echo in Deut. 4:12 showing God's began speaking the commandments directly, until they asked that Moses be the one to speak to them instead (Exodus 20:18-19).

De 4:21 Furthermore Yahweh was angry with me for your sakes, and swore that I should not go over the Jordan, and that I should not go in to that good land which Yahweh your God gives you for an inheritance; **22** but I must die in this land. I must not go over the Jordan; **but you shall go over, and possess that good land**. **23** Take heed to yourselves, lest you forget the covenant of Yahweh your God, which he made with you, and make yourselves a carved image in the form of anything which Yahweh your God has forbidden you. **24** For Yahweh your God is a devouring fire, a jealous God.

25 When you shall father children and children's children, **and you shall have been long in the land, and shall corrupt yourselves, and make a carved image in the form of anything, and shall do that which is evil** in Yahweh your God's sight to provoke him to anger, **26** I call heaven and earth to witness against you today, that you will soon utterly perish from off the land which you go over the Jordan to possess it. You will not prolong your days on it, but will utterly be destroyed.

2Cor 3:4 Such **confidence we have through Christ** toward God, 5 not that we are sufficient of ourselves to account anything as from ourselves; but our sufficiency is from God,

De 4:27 Yahweh will scatter you among the peoples, and **you will be left few in number** among the nations where Yahweh will lead you away. **28** There you will **serve** gods, the work of men's hands, wood and stone, which neither see, nor hear, nor eat, nor smell. **29** But from there you shall seek Yahweh your God, and you will find him when you search after him with all your heart and with all your soul. **30** When you are in oppression, and all these things have come on you, in the latter days you shall return to Yahweh your God and listen to his voice. **31** For Yahweh your God is a merciful God. He will not fail you nor destroy you, nor forget the **covenant** of your fathers which he swore to them.

32 For ask now of the days that are past, which were before you, since the day that God created man on the earth, and from the one end of the sky to the other, whether there has been anything as great as this thing, or has been heard like it? **33 Did a people ever hear the voice of God speaking out of the middle of the fire, as you have heard, and live**? **34** Or has God tried to go and take a nation for himself from among another nation, by trials, by signs, by wonders, by war, by a mighty hand, by an outstretched arm, and by great terrors, according to all that Yahweh your God did for you in Egypt before your eyes? **35** It was shown to you so that you might know that Yahweh is God. There is no one else besides him. **36** Out of heaven he made you to hear his voice, that he might instruct you. On earth he made you to see his great fire; and you heard his words out of the middle of the fire. **37** Because he loved your fathers, therefore he chose their offspring after them, and brought you out with his presence, with his great power, out of Egypt; **38** to drive out nations from before you greater and mightier than you, to bring you in, to give you their land for an inheritance, as it is today. **39** Know therefore today, and take it to heart, that Yahweh himself is God in heaven above and on the earth beneath. There is no one else. **40** You shall keep his statutes and his commandments which I command you today, that it may go well with you and with your children after you, and that you may prolong your days in the land which Yahweh your God gives you for all time.

2**Cor 3:6** who also **made us sufficient** as **servants** of a new **covenant**, not of the letter but of the Spirit. **For the letter kills, but the Spirit gives life**.

NOTE: This is the first of just two mentions of the word *covenant* in 2 Corinthians, the second is in 2 Cor. 3:14. While his forefathers were scattered into Babylon, left few in number forced to serve other gods, Paul speaks of *willingly* leaving the land of Israel, few in number but *sufficient* in God for the task of *serving* the work of new *covenant*, not of the letter but God speaking directly, as from fire, that gives life.

De 4:41 Then Moses set apart three cities beyond the Jordan toward the sunrise, **42** that the manslayer might flee there, who kills his neighbor unintentionally and didn't hate him in time past, and that fleeing to one of these cities he might live: **43** Bezer in the wilderness, in the plain country, for the Reubenites; and Ramoth in Gilead for the Gadites; and Golan in Bashan for the Manassites.

44 This is the law which Moses set before the children of Israel. **45** These are the testimonies, and the statutes, and the ordinances which Moses spoke to the children of Israel when they came out of Egypt, **46** beyond the Jordan, in the valley over against Beth Peor, in the land of Sihon king of the Amorites, who lived at Heshbon, whom Moses and the children of Israel struck when they came out of Egypt. **47** They took possession of his land and the land of Og king of Bashan, the two kings of the Amorites, who were beyond the Jordan toward the sunrise; **48** from Aroer, which is on the edge of the valley of the Arnon, even to Mount Sion (also called Hermon), **49** and all the Arabah beyond the Jordan eastward, even to the sea of the Arabah, under the slopes of Pisgah.

NOTE: These verses seem to be skipped by Paul.

Deuteronomy 5	2 Cor. 3:7

De 5:1 Moses called to all Israel, and said to them, "Hear, Israel, the statutes and the ordinances which I speak in your ears today, that you may learn them, and observe to do them." **2** Yahweh our **God made a covenant with us in Horeb**. **3** Yahweh didn't make this covenant with our fathers, but with us, even us, who are all of us here alive today. **4** **Yahweh spoke with you face to face on the mountain out of the middle of the fire**, **5** (I stood between Yahweh and you at that time, to show you Yahweh's word, for you were afraid because of the fire, and didn't go up onto the mountain), saying,

2**Cor 3:7a** But if the service of death, **written engraved on stones**, **came with glory**, so that the children of Israel could not look steadfastly on the face of Moses

De 5:6 "I am Yahweh your God, who brought you out of the land of Egypt, out of the house of bondage.

7 You shall have no other gods before me.

8 You shall not make a carved image for yourself—any likeness of what is in heaven above, or what is in the earth beneath, or that is in the water under the earth. **9** You shall not bow down to them nor serve them; for I, Yahweh your God, am a jealous God, visiting the iniquity of the fathers on the children and on the third and on the fourth generation of those who hate me, **10** and showing loving kindness to thousands of those who love me and keep my commandments.

11 You shall not take the name of Yahweh your God in vain, for Yahweh will not hold him guiltless who takes his name in vain.

12 Observe the Sabbath day, to keep it holy, as Yahweh your God commanded you. **13** You shall labor six days, and do all your work; **14** but the seventh day is a Sabbath to Yahweh your God, in which you shall not do any work—you, nor your son, nor your daughter, nor your male servant, nor your female servant, nor your ox, nor your donkey, nor any of your livestock, nor your stranger who is within your gates; that your male servant and your female servant may rest as well as you. **15** You shall remember that you were a servant in the land of Egypt, and Yahweh your God brought you out of there by a mighty hand and by an outstretched arm. Therefore Yahweh your God commanded you to keep the Sabbath day.

16 Honor your father and your mother, as Yahweh your God commanded you, that your days may be long, and that it may go well with you in the land which Yahweh your God gives you.

17 You shall not murder.

18 Neither shall you commit adultery.

19 Neither shall you steal.

20 Neither shall you give false testimony against your neighbor.

21 Neither shall you covet your neighbor's wife. Neither shall you desire your neighbor's house, his field, or his male servant, or his female servant, his ox, or his donkey, or anything that is your neighbor's."

NOTE: Here, Paul seems to be focused on the giving of the Torah as a whole, so he does not echo any of the Ten Commandments specifically.

De 5:22 These words Yahweh spoke to all your assembly on the mountain out of the middle of the fire, of the cloud, and of the thick darkness, with a great voice. He added no more. He wrote them on two stone tablets, **and gave them to me**.

2Cor 3:7b **for the glory of his face, which was passing away**,

NOTE: After the initial experience at Horeb, for the next forty years it would be Moses' face that would show the residual glory of that event. That glory would only last while Moses lived.

De 5:23 When you heard the voice out of the middle of the darkness, while the mountain was burning with fire, you came near to me, even all the heads of your tribes, and your elders; **24** and you said, **"Behold, Yahweh our God has shown us his glory and his greatness, and we have heard his voice out of the middle of the fire. We have seen today that God does speak with man, and he lives**. **25** Now therefore, why should we die? For this great fire will consume us. If we hear Yahweh our God's voice any more, then we shall die. **26** For who is there of all flesh who has heard the voice of the living God speaking out of the middle of the fire, as we have, and lived? **27** Go near, and hear all that Yahweh our God shall say, and tell us all that Yahweh our God tells you; and we will hear it, and do it."

28 Yahweh heard the voice of your words when you spoke to me; and Yahweh said to me, "*I have heard the voice of the words of this people which they have spoken to you. They have well said all that they have spoken*. **29** Oh that there were such a heart in them that they would fear me and keep all my commandments always, that it might be well with them and with their children forever! **30** Go tell them, 'Return to your tents.' **31** But as for you, stand here by me, and I will tell you all the commandments, and the statutes, and the ordinances, which you shall teach them, that they may do them in the land which I give them to possess." **32** You shall observe to do therefore as Yahweh your God has commanded you. You shall not turn away to the right hand or to the left. **33** You shall walk in all the way which Yahweh your God has commanded you, that you may live and that it may be well with you, and that you may prolong your days in the land which you shall possess.

2Cor 3:8 won't service of the Spirit be with much more glory?

9 For if the service of condemnation *has glory*, the service of righteousness exceeds much more in glory. **10** For most certainly that which has been made glorious has not been made glorious in this respect, by reason of the glory that surpasses. **11** For if that which passes away was with glory, much more that which remains is in glory.

NOTE: God's initial encounter with the people at Sinai was with great glory (echo 1). But the people condemned this kind of interaction and asked that Moses go to God directly and then they would obey whatever God tells Moses (echo 2). But God said that in this request they had spoken well, giving it glory (echo 3). But the service of righteousness is that God invited Moses to stand next to God, so the glory seen by Moses far surpasses the glory of what people saw on the face of Moses. (echo 4).

NOTE: These points are emphasized again in 2 Corinthians 3:10: The glory of the people seeing the glory of God was surpassed by the glory of Moses standing by God. In 2 Cor. 3:11, the people did not see the glory of God at Mount Sinai again because of their decision to ask Moses to meet with God without them, only the glory of the face of Moses. However, even though that glory passed away when Moses died, it does not decrease in any way the glory that remains in God's presence, which is the glory for which Paul hopes. This is further developed in 2 Cor. 3:18.

Deuteronomy 6

2 Cor. 3:12

De 6:1 Now these are the commandments, the statutes, and the ordinances, which Yahweh your God commanded to teach you, that you might do them in the land where you go over to possess it, **2** that you might fear Yahweh your God, to keep all his statutes and his commandments, which I command you—you, your son, and your son's son, all the days of your life; and that your days may be prolonged. **3** Hear therefore, Israel, and observe to do it, that it may be well with you, and that you may increase mightily, as Yahweh, the God of your fathers, has promised to you, in a land flowing with milk and honey.

4 **Hear, Israel: Yahweh is our God. Yahweh is one**. **5** You shall love Yahweh your God with all your heart, with all your soul, and with all your might.

2**Cor 3:12**
Having therefore such a hope, we use great **boldness in our speech**.

NOTE: Deuteronomy 6:4, the Shema is one of the boldest statements in the Judaism. An untold number of Jews through the ages have chosen to die rather than to agree that anyone or anything else is God.

De 6:6 <u>These words, which I command you today, shall be on your heart</u>; **7** and you shall teach them diligently to your children, and shall talk of them when you sit in your house, and when you walk by the way, and when you lie down, and when you rise up. **8** You shall bind them for a sign on your hand, and they shall be for frontlets between your eyes. **9** You shall write them on the door posts of your house and on your gates.

10 It shall be, when Yahweh your God brings you into the land which he swore to your fathers, to Abraham, to Isaac, and to Jacob, to give you, great and goodly cities which you didn't build, **11** and houses full of all good things which you didn't fill, and cisterns dug out which you didn't dig, vineyards and olive trees which you didn't plant, and you shall eat and be full; **12** then beware lest you forget Yahweh, who brought you out of the land of Egypt, out of the house of bondage. **13** You shall fear Yahweh your God; and you shall serve him, and shall swear by his name. **14** You shall not go after other gods, of the gods of the peoples who are around you, **15** for Yahweh your God among you is a jealous God, lest the anger of Yahweh your God be kindled against you, and he destroy you from off the face of the earth.

2Cor 2:13 and not as **<u>Moses, who put a veil on his face, that the children of Israel wouldn't look steadfastly on the end of that which was passing away</u>**.

NOTE: When Moses was speaking these words to the Children of Israel in Deuteronomy 6:6 it seems that Moses still wore a veil. The words "command you today" were also spoken by Moses in Exodus 34:11 the second time that he brought the tablets down from the mountain, and were immediately followed by the account of his face having shown. Paul it seems shifts his focus from Deuteronomy to Ex. 34: 29-35. Therefore the next sectional pairing pairs these same verses of 2 Corinthians 13-16 with the corresponding verses in Exodus. We call this the Exodus interlude.

Exodus Interlude (6 verses only)   2 Cor. 3:13

EXODUS 34:29-35.

34:29 When **Moses** came down from Mount Sinai with the two tablets of the covenant in Moses' hand, when he came down from the mountain, Moses didn't know that the skin of his face shone by reason of his speaking with him. **30** When Aaron and all the children of Israel saw Moses, behold, the skin of his face shone; and they were afraid to come near him. **31** Moses called to them, and Aaron and all the rulers of the congregation returned to him; and Moses spoke to them. **32** Afterward all the children of Israel came near, and he gave them all the commandments that Yahweh had spoken with him on Mount Sinai. **33** When Moses was done speaking with them, he put a <u>veil</u> on his face. **34** But when Moses went in before Yahweh to speak with him, he took the *veil* off, until he came out; and he came out, and spoke to the children of Israel that which he was commanded. **35** The children of Israel saw Moses' face, that the skin of Moses' face shone; so Moses put the <u>veil</u> on his face again, <u>until he went</u> in to speak with him.

2**Cor 3:13** and not as **Moses**, who put a <u>veil</u> on his face, that the children of Israel wouldn't look steadfastly on the end of that which was passing away. **14** But their minds were hardened, for until this very day at the reading of the old covenant the same *veil* remains, because in Christ it passes away. **15** But to this day, when Moses is read, a <u>veil</u> lies on their heart. **16** But whenever someone turns to the Lord, the <u>veil</u> is taken away.

NOTE: Each of these passages has four references to the veil. The first three in Exodus are explicit, and the fourth is implied by the words "until he went." The fourth reference from Paul speaks of this when he writes "But whenever someone turns to the Lord, the veil is taken away." Having echoed 2 Corinthians 3:13-16 against this short passage in Exodus, Paul returns to Deuteronomy to outline the rest of his letter.

Deuteronomy 6:16

6:16 You shall not tempt Yahweh your God, as you tempted him in Massah. **17** You shall diligently keep the commandments of Yahweh your God, and his testimonies, and his statutes, which he has commanded you. **18** You shall do that which is right and good in Yahweh's sight, that it may be well with you and that you may go in and possess the good land which Yahweh swore to your fathers, **19** to thrust out all your enemies from before you, as Yahweh has spoken.

20 When your son asks you in time to come, saying, "What do the testimonies, the statutes, and the ordinances, which Yahweh our God has commanded you mean?" **21** then you shall tell your son, "We were Pharaoh's slaves in Egypt. **Yahweh brought us out of Egypt** with a mighty hand; **22** and *Yahweh showed great and awesome signs and wonders on Egypt, on Pharaoh, and on all his house, before our eyes*; **23** and he brought us out from there, that he might bring us in, to give us the land which he swore to our fathers. **24** Yahweh commanded us to do all these statutes, **to fear Yahweh our God, for our good always, that he might preserve us alive, as we are today**. **25** It shall be righteousness to us, if we observe to do all this commandment **before Yahweh our God**, as he has commanded us."

2Cor 3:17 Now the Lord is the Spirit and **where the Spirit of the Lord is, there is liberty**.

18 But *we all, with unveiled face seeing the glory of the Lord as in a mirror*, are **transformed into the same image from glory** to glory, even **as from the Lord, the Spirit**.

NOTE: The story of the Exodus was a story of liberty (echo 1). The great and awesome signs and wonders were said to be "before our eyes," echoing "with unveiled face seeing the glory of the Lord," yet not directly, but rather "as in a mirror," (echo 2). They are "preserved alive, we are today," echoes today's "glory," (echo 3). But the righteousness in the future, "if they observe and do all" is a "glory" of the future (echo 4). Notice that in the final echo is the phrase "before Yahweh our God" hints at directly seeing his glory.

NOTE: 2 Corinthians 3:18 may also be viewed as a summary echo of Exodus 34:29-35. See Exodus Interlude in the previous section.

Deuteronomy 7 | 2 Cor. 4

De 7:1 When Yahweh your God brings you into the land where you go to possess it, and casts out many nations before you—the Hittite, the Girgashite, the Amorite, the Canaanite, the Perizzite, the Hivite, and the Jebusite—seven nations greater and mightier than you, **2** and when Yahweh your God delivers them up before you, and you **strike them, then you shall utterly destroy them**. You shall make no covenant with them, nor show mercy to them. **3 You shall not make marriages with them. You shall not give your daughter to his son, nor shall you take his daughter for your son**. **4** For that would turn away your sons from following me, that they may serve other gods. So Yahweh's anger would be kindled against you, and he would destroy you quickly. **5** But you shall deal with them like this: you shall break down their altars, dash their pillars in pieces, cut down their Asherah poles, and burn their engraved images with fire. **6** *For you are a holy people to Yahweh your God*. Yahweh your God has chosen you to be a people for his own possession, above all peoples who are on the face of the earth.

7 Yahweh didn't set his love on you nor choose you because you were more in number than any people; for you were the fewest of all peoples; **8** but because Yahweh loves you, and because he would keep the oath which he swore to your fathers, Yahweh has brought you out with a mighty hand and redeemed you out of the house of bondage, from the hand of Pharaoh king of Egypt. **9** Know therefore that Yahweh your God himself is God, the faithful God, who keeps covenant and loving kindness with them who love him and keep his commandments to a thousand generations, **10** and repays those who hate him **to their face, to destroy them**. He will not be slack to **him who hates him; he will repay him to his face**. **11** You shall therefore keep the commandments, the statutes, and the ordinances which I command you today, to do them.

2**Cor 4:1** Therefore, seeing we have this ministry, even as we obtained mercy, **we don't faint**. **2** But **we have renounced the hidden things of shame**, not walking in craftiness **nor handling the word of God deceitfully**, but by the manifestation of the *truth commending ourselves to every man's conscience* in the sight of God.

3 Even if our Good News is veiled, it is veiled in those who are dying, **4** in whom the god of this world **has blinded the minds of the unbelieving**, that the light of the Good News of the glory of Christ, who is the image of God, should not dawn on them.

NOTE: [Va'etchanan ends.] In this pairing both Deuteronomy and 2 Corinthians clearly undergo a sharp change in tone. In 2 Corinthians 4:2 the phrase "not walking in craftiness" is suggested to echo the phrase "make no covenant with them" in Deuteronomy 7:2 because the Gibeonites would soon make a covenant deceitfully with Israel in Joshua Ch. 9. The phrase "handling the word of God deceitfully" in 2 Cor. 4:2 can also be translated as "adulterating the word of God," and echoes Deut. 7:3 "you shall not make marriages with them." In 2 Cor. 4:4 "blinded" seems to echo "face" in Deut. 7:10.

Deuteronomy 7:12 | ## 2 Corinthians 4:5

De 7:12 It shall happen, **because you listen to these ordinances** and keep and do them, that Yahweh your God will keep with you <u>the covenant and the loving kindness</u> which he swore to your fathers. **13** He will love you, bless you, and multiply you. He will also bless the fruit of your body and the fruit of your ground, your grain and your new wine and **your oil**, the increase of your livestock and the young of your flock, in the land which he swore to your fathers to give you. **14** *You will be blessed above all peoples*. There will not be male or female barren among you, or among your livestock. **15** <u>**Yahweh will take away from you all sickness; and he will put none of the evil diseases of Egypt, which you know, on you, but will lay them on all those who hate you**</u>. **16** <u>**You shall consume all the peoples whom Yahweh your God shall deliver to you**</u>. Your eye shall not pity them. You shall not serve their gods; for that would be a snare to you.

2Cor 4:5 For we don't **preach** ourselves, but <u>Christ Jesus as Lord</u>, and ourselves as your servants for Jesus' sake, **6** seeing it is God who said, "<u>**Light will shine**</u> out of darkness," who has shone in our hearts to give the light of the knowledge of the glory of God in the face of Jesus Christ.

7 But we have this *treasure in clay vessels*, that the **exceeding greatness of the power may be of God** and not from ourselves.

NOTE: [Eikev.] The "covenant and loving kindness" is God's work alone! Thus, Paul preaches not himself but only God's work alone, which is "Christ Jesus as Lord." Paul, in his final echo, not only sees the power of God to remove all sickness, but in the final phrase "whom Yahweh your God shall deliver to you," sees a picture **of the entire world coming into a saving knowledge of Jesus Christ**. "Consuming all the peoples" is not about destruction, but overwhelming the darkness with light. As written in 2 Cor. 4:6, that light is the "light of the knowledge of the glory of God in the face of Jesus Christ. See also the note below 2 Cor. 2:14 regarding the conquests of Israel.

De 7:17 If you shall say in your heart, "These nations are more than I; how can I dispossess them?" **18** you shall not be afraid of them. You shall remember well what Yahweh your God did to Pharaoh and to all Egypt: **19** the great trials which your eyes saw, the signs, the wonders, the mighty hand, and the outstretched arm, by which Yahweh your God brought you out. So shall Yahweh your God do to all the peoples of whom you are afraid. **20** Moreover Yahweh your God will send the hornet among them, until those who are left, and hide themselves, perish from before you. **21** You shall not be scared of them; for Yahweh your God is among you, a great and awesome God. **22** Yahweh your God will cast out those nations before you little by little. You may not consume them at once, lest the animals of the field increase on you. **23** But Yahweh your God **will deliver them up before you, and will confuse them with a great confusion**, until they are destroyed.

24 He will deliver their kings into your hand, and you shall make their name perish from under the sky. **No one will be able to stand before you until you have destroyed them**. **25** You shall burn the engraved images of their gods with fire. **You shall not covet the silver or the gold that is on them, nor take it for yourself, lest you be snared in it; for it is an abomination to Yahweh your God. 26 You shall not bring an abomination into your house** and become a devoted thing like it. You shall utterly detest it. You shall utterly abhor it; for it is a devoted thing.

2**Cor 4:8** We are pressed on every side, yet not crushed;

perplexed, yet not to despair;

9 pursued, yet not forsaken; **struck down, yet not destroyed**; **10** always **carrying in the body the putting to death of the Lord Jesus**, that the life of Jesus may also be revealed in our body.

11 For we who live are always delivered to death for Jesus' sake, that the life also of Jesus may be revealed in our mortal flesh. **12** So then death works in us, but life in you.

NOTE: Paul seems to take keywords from the Deuteronomy account of their concern for the difficult tasks ahead of them, and uses those words to discuss their actual hardships, yet the hope within them. Pharaoh and Egypt *pressed* Israel on every side (echo 1). *Confusion* echoes *perplexed* (echo 2). Delivered echoes pursued (echo 3). *Not able to stand* echoes *struck down* and *destroyed* echoes *destroyed* (echo 4). Finally, *coveting* is a sin that can happen any time day or night, thus it must be put to death continually in one's self.

Deuteronomy 8

2 Cor. 4:13

De 8:1 You shall observe to do all the commandments which I command you today, that you may live, and multiply, and go in and possess the land which Yahweh swore to your fathers. **2** You shall remember all the way which Yahweh your God has led you these forty years in the wilderness, that he might humble you, to test you, to know what was in your heart, whether you would keep his commandments or not. **3** He humbled you, allowed you to hunger, and fed you with manna, which you didn't know, neither did your fathers know; that he might teach you that man does not live by bread only, but man lives by every word that proceeds out of Yahweh's mouth. **4** Your clothing didn't grow old on you, neither did your foot swell, these forty years. **5** You shall consider in your heart that as a man disciplines his son, so Yahweh your God disciplines you. **6** You shall keep the commandments of Yahweh your God, to walk in his ways, and to fear him. **7** For Yahweh your God brings you into a good land, a land of brooks of water, of springs, and underground water flowing into valleys and hills; **8** a land of wheat, barley, vines, fig trees, and pomegranates; a land of olive trees and honey; **9** a land in which you shall eat bread without scarcity, you shall not lack anything in it; a land whose stones are iron, and out of whose hills you may dig copper. **10** You shall eat and be full, and you shall bless Yahweh your God for the good land which he has given you.

2Cor 4:13 But having the same spirit of faith, according to that which is written, "I believed, and therefore I spoke." We also believe, and therefore we also speak, **14** knowing that he who raised the Lord Jesus will raise us also with Jesus, and will present us with you.

15 For all things are for your sakes, **that the grace, being multiplied through the many, may cause the thanksgiving to abound to the glory of God**.

NOTE: In the first echo, Paul is saying that true living from the mouth of God is to be god-like in our own speech! That this is how we find proof of God words being our bread! In the second echo, our being multiplied through "the many" is pictured in the entire nation of Israel being blessed by God.

De 8:11 Beware lest you forget Yahweh your God, in not keeping his commandments, his ordinances, and his statutes, which I command you today; **12** lest, when you have eaten and are full, and have built fine houses and lived in them; **13** and when your herds and your flocks multiply, and your silver and your gold is multiplied, and all that you have is multiplied; **14** then your heart might be lifted up, and you forget Yahweh your God, who brought you out of the land of Egypt, out of the house of bondage; **15** who led you through the great and terrible wilderness, with venomous snakes and scorpions, and thirsty ground where there was no water; who brought you water out of the rock of flint; **16** who fed you in the wilderness with manna, which your fathers didn't know, that he might humble you, and that he might test you, to do you good at your latter end; **17** and lest you say in your heart, "<u>My power and the might of my hand has gotten me this wealth</u>." **18 But you shall remember Yahweh your God, for it is he who gives you power to get wealth, that he may establish his covenant which he swore to your fathers**, as it is today. **19** It shall be, if you shall forget Yahweh your God, and walk after other gods, and serve them and worship them, I testify against you today that you shall surely perish. **20** As the nations that Yahweh makes to perish before you, so you shall perish, because you wouldn't listen to Yahweh your God's voice.

2Cor 4:16 Therefore we don't faint, but though **<u>our outward person is decaying</u>**, **yet our inward person is renewed day by day**.

NOTE: The warning of Moses in this passage to Israel is the danger of letting physical success allow a sin of the heart. Paul counters this idea by reminding the Corinthians that the outward person – the person that is impacted by physical things – is decaying continually, but that the inward person – the place where sin can lodge, can be renewed daily, not allowing the sin to lodge. But Paul has another point to make in the very next pairing.

Deuteronomy 9   2 Cor. 4:17

De 9:1 Hear, Israel! You are to pass over the Jordan today, to go in to dispossess nations greater and mightier than yourself, cities great and fortified up to the sky, **2** a people great and tall, the sons of the Anakim, whom you know, and of whom you have heard say, "**Who can stand before the sons of Anak**?" **3** Know therefore today that Yahweh your God is he who goes over before you as a **devouring fire**. He will destroy them, and he will bring them down before you. So you shall drive them out and make them perish quickly, as Yahweh has spoken to you.

4 Don't say in your heart, after Yahweh your God has thrust them out from before you, "For my righteousness Yahweh has brought me in to possess this land"; because Yahweh drives them out before you because of the wickedness of these nations. **5** Not for your righteousness or for the uprightness of your heart do you go in to possess their land; but for the wickedness of these nations Yahweh your God does drive them out from before you, and **that he may establish the word which Yahweh swore to your fathers**, to Abraham, to Isaac, and to Jacob.

2Cor 4:17 For **our light affliction, which is for the moment**, works for us more and more exceedingly an **eternal weight of glory, 18** while we don't look at the things which are seen, but at the things which are not seen. For the things which are seen are temporal, but **the things which are not seen are eternal**.

NOTE: Continuing… but the affliction we experience when we engage in the service of God's kingdom, works positively for us, forcing us to look at the things which are unseen, because they are eternal.

NOTE: The pillar of fire would no longer be seen over the Children of Israel, but it would essentially "go over before them" into the promised land. Paul echoes this idea in the phrase "eternal weight of glory." Regarding the final echo, God's *Word* is *eternal* according to Isaiah 40:8.

Deuteronomy 9:6	2 Cor. 5

De 9:6 Know therefore that Yahweh your God doesn't give you this good land to possess for your righteousness, for you are a stiff-necked people. 7 Remember, and don't forget, how you provoked Yahweh your God to wrath in the wilderness. From the day that you left the land of Egypt until you came to this place, you have been rebellious against Yahweh. 8 Also in Horeb you provoked Yahweh to wrath, and **Yahweh was angry with you to destroy you**. 9 <u>When I had gone up onto the mountain to receive the stone tablets, even the tablets of the covenant which Yahweh made with you, then I stayed on the mountain forty days and forty nights</u>. I neither ate bread nor drank water. 10 Yahweh delivered to me the two stone tablets written with God's finger. On them were all the words which Yahweh spoke with you on the mountain out of the middle of the fire in the day of the assembly. 11 It came to pass at the end of forty days and forty nights that Yahweh gave me the two stone tablets, even the tablets of the covenant. 12 Yahweh said to me, "<u>Arise, get down quickly from here; for your people whom you have brought out of Egypt have corrupted themselves</u>. They have quickly turned away from the way which I commanded them. They have made a **molten image** for themselves!" 13 Furthermore Yahweh spoke to me, saying, "I have seen this people, and behold, they are a stiff-necked people. 14 Leave me alone, that I may destroy them, **and blot out their name from under the sky; and I will make of you a nation mightier and greater than they.**"

2Cor 5:1 For we know that if the **earthly house of our tent is dissolved**, we have a building from God, <u>**a house not made with hands, eternal, in the heavens**</u>. 2 For most certainly in this we groan, longing to be clothed with our habitation which is from heaven,

3 <u>if indeed being clothed, we will not be found naked</u>. 4 For indeed we who are in this tent do groan, being burdened, not that we desire to be unclothed, but that we desire to be **clothed, that what is mortal may be swallowed up by life**.

NOTE: In the first echo, remember that when Moses speaks these words, the people of God are all together with him standing in view of the tabernacle. Moses' words are harsh, saying they have been rebellious and stiff-necked. Indeed, the future temple would be destroyed, but the promises of God to them were not nullified. Paul echoes this by seeing that even if our physical body is destroyed (a temple of the H.S. in 1 Corinthians 6:19), there is a place for us in the heavens. In the third echo, the people corrupting of themselves is pictured in their removal of their clothing. The fourth echo explains Paul's use of clothed vs. unclothed in that the term "molten image" is made by the pouring out of metal as a covering over the idol. He takes that thought and redeems it though the covering of Christ! The final echo show us that in Christ we are not only covered, but we are swallowed up in life – an idea so glorious as to be practically beyond all comprehension.

De 9:15 So I turned and <u>came down from the mountain, and the mountain was burning with fire</u>. The two tablets of the covenant were in my two hands. **16** I looked, and behold, you had sinned against Yahweh your God. You had made yourselves a molten calf. You had quickly turned away from the way which Yahweh had commanded you. **17** I took hold of the two tablets, and threw them out of my two hands, and broke them before your eyes. **18** I fell down before Yahweh, as at the first, forty days and forty nights. I neither ate bread nor drank water, because of all your sin which you sinned, in doing that which was evil in Yahweh's sight, to provoke him to anger. **19** For I was afraid of the anger and hot displeasure with which Yahweh was angry against you to destroy you. But Yahweh listened to me that time also. **20** Yahweh was angry enough with Aaron to destroy him. I prayed for Aaron also at the same time. **21 I took your sin, the calf which you had made, and burned it with fire, and crushed it, grinding it very small, until it was as fine as dust. I threw its dust into the brook that descended out of the mountain.**

2Cor 5:5 Now he who made us for this very thing is God, who also gave to us the down payment **of the Spirit**.

6 Therefore we are always confident and know that while we are at home in the body, we are absent from the Lord, **7** for **we walk by faith, not by sight**.

NOTE: The Holy Spirit, sent from heaven, baptizes us in fire -- a down payment of the life that is to come when we are with Christ in the heavenlies. The term "down payment" here is perhaps better translated as "pledge." In the last echo, nowhere in the Bible does it say that God commanded Moses to grind up the golden calf as fine as dust and throw it into the brook. It seems that Paul sees in those described actions that Moses walked by faith, not by sight.

De 9:22 At Taberah, at Massah, and at Kibroth Hattaavah you provoked Yahweh to wrath. **23** When **Yahweh sent you from Kadesh Barnea, saying, "Go up and possess the land which I have given you**," you rebelled against the commandment of Yahweh your God, and you didn't believe him, nor listen to his voice. **24** You have been rebellious against Yahweh from the day that I knew you.

25 So I fell down before Yahweh the forty days and forty nights that I fell down, because Yahweh had said he would destroy you. **26** I prayed to Yahweh, and said, "Lord Yahweh, don't destroy your people and your inheritance that you have redeemed through your greatness, that you have brought out of Egypt with a mighty hand. **27** Remember your servants, Abraham, Isaac, and Jacob. Don't look at the stubbornness of this people, nor at their wickedness, nor at their sin, **28** lest the land you brought us out from say, 'Because Yahweh was not able to bring them into the land which he promised to them, and because he hated them, he has brought them out to kill them in the wilderness.' **29** Yet they are your people and your inheritance, which you brought out by your great power and by your outstretched arm."

2Cor **5:8** We are courageous, I say, and are willing rather **to be absent from the body and to be at home with the Lord**. **9** Therefore also we make it our aim, whether at home or absent, to be well pleasing to him.

10 For we must all be revealed before the judgment seat of Christ that **each one may receive the things in the body, according to what he has done**, whether good or bad.

NOTE: In the first echo, the people of God were forced by God to remain in the wilderness for forty years, even though God had said they could "go up" and possess the land that He had given them. Those men, while they lived out the rest of their lives in the wilderness, could never enter the promised land. Only in their deaths could they experience that potential for the fullness of presence with God. In the same way, we live out our lives in the wilderness, but when we depart this life, we experience the fulness as well. In the second echo, is it possible that Moses was praying to God while Christ was sitting in judgment over the people. In the third echo, the good works of the three servants of God were contrasted with the stubbornness of the people, but Paul assures that the judgement, whether good or bad, is fair.

Deuteronomy 10

2 Corinthians 5:11

De 10:1 At that time Yahweh said to me, "Cut two stone tablets like the first, and **come up to me onto the mountain**, and make an ark of wood. 2 I will write on the tablets the words that were on the first tablets which you broke, and you shall put them in the ark." **3 So I made an ark of acacia wood, and cut two stone tablets like the first, and went up onto the mountain, having the two tablets in my hand**. **4 He wrote on the tablets, according to the first writing, the ten commandments**, which Yahweh spoke to you on the mountain out of the middle of the fire in the day of the assembly; and Yahweh gave them to me. 5 I turned and came down from the mountain, and put the tablets in the ark which I had made; and they are there, as Yahweh commanded me.

6 (*The children of Israel traveled from the wells of the children of Jaakan to Moserah. There Aaron died*, and there he was buried; and Eleazar his son ministered in the priest's office in his place. 7 From there they traveled to Gudgodah; and from Gudgodah to Jotbathah, a land of brooks of water. **8 At that time Yahweh set apart the tribe of Levi to bear the ark of Yahweh's covenant, to stand before Yahweh to minister to him**, and to bless in his name, to this day. 9 Therefore Levi has no portion nor inheritance with his brothers; Yahweh is his inheritance, according as Yahweh your God spoke to him.)

2Cor 5:11 Knowing therefore the fear of the Lord, we persuade men, but **we are revealed to God**, and I hope that we are revealed also in your consciences. 12 For we are not commending ourselves to you again, but speak as giving you occasion of boasting on our behalf, that you may have something to answer those who boast in appearance, and not in heart. **13 For if we are beside ourselves, it is for God**. Or if we are of sober mind, it is for you. 14 For the love of Christ constrains us; because we are persuaded that one died for all, therefore all died.

15 *He died for all*, that **those who live should no longer live to themselves, but to him who for their sakes died** and rose again.

NOTE: Regarding "Aaron died," in Deuteronomy 10:6, Paul would not echo Aaron "the man" to Christ, but rather the "office of high priest." Christ as priest died for us to reconcile us to himself, the very point that Paul is about to make in verse 18.

De 10:10 **I stayed on the mountain, as at the first time, forty days and forty nights; and Yahweh listened to me that time also**. Yahweh would not destroy you. **11** Yahweh said to me, "<u>Arise, take your journey before the people; and they shall go in and possess the land which I swore to their fathers to give to them.</u>"

2Cor 5:16 Therefore **we know no one according to the flesh from now on**. Even though we have known Christ according to the flesh, yet now we know him so no more. **17** <u>Therefore if anyone is in Christ, he is a new creation. The old things have passed away. Behold, all things have become new</u>.

De 10:12 Now, Israel, what does Yahweh your God require of you, but to fear Yahweh your God, to walk in all his ways, to love him, and to serve Yahweh your God with all your heart and with all your soul, **13** to keep the commandments of Yahweh, and his statutes, which I command you today for your good? 14 Behold, **to Yahweh your God belongs the heaven, the heaven of heavens, and the earth, with all that is in it**. 15 Only Yahweh had a delight in your fathers to love them, and he chose their offspring after them, even you above all peoples, as it is today. 16 Circumcise therefore the foreskin of your heart and be no more stiff-necked. 17 For Yahweh your God, he is God of gods and Lord of lords, the great God, the mighty, and the awesome, who doesn't respect persons or take bribes. 18 He executes justice for the fatherless and widow, and loves the foreigner in giving him food and clothing. 19 <u>Therefore love the foreigner, for you were foreigners in the land of Egypt</u>. 20 You shall fear Yahweh your God. You shall serve him, and you shall cling to him, and you shall swear by his name. 21 He is your praise, and he is your God, who has done for you these great and awesome things which your eyes have seen. 22 <u>Your fathers went down into Egypt with seventy persons</u>; and now Yahweh your God has made you as the stars of the sky for multitude.

2Cor 5:18 **But all things are of God**, who reconciled us to himself through Jesus Christ, and **gave to us the ministry of reconciliation**; 19 namely, that <u>God was in Christ reconciling the world to himself</u>, not reckoning to them their trespasses, and having committed to us the word of reconciliation.

NOTE: Up until this point, Moses has been stressing the need for righteousness and not to be corrupted by the people of the land. Now he turns to the foreigner who enters their land, and asks that love be shown to them. Paul sees this as an echo of God's ministry of reconciliation. In the last echo, the number *seventy* is equated with the number of nations of the world (Genesis Ch. 10). God's plan in sending the seventy to Egypt was not just to "bring them out" but to provide a plan and picture of deliverance of the entire world from the slavery of sin (Gen. 46:27).

Deuteronomy 11   2 Cor. 5:20

De 11:1 Therefore you shall love Yahweh your God, and keep his instructions, his statutes, his ordinances, and his commandments, always. **2** Know this day—for I don't speak with your children who have not known, and who haven't seen the chastisement of Yahweh your God, his greatness, his mighty hand, his outstretched arm, **3** his signs, and his works, which he did in the middle of Egypt to Pharaoh the king of Egypt, and to all his land; **4** and what he did to the army of Egypt, to their horses, and to their chariots; how he made the water of the Red Sea to overflow them as they pursued you, and how Yahweh has destroyed them to this day; **5** and what he did to you in the wilderness until you came to this place; **6** and what he did to Dathan and Abiram, the sons of Eliab, the son of Reuben—how the earth opened its mouth and swallowed them up, with their households, their tents, and every living thing that followed them, in the middle of all Israel; **7** but your eyes have seen all of Yahweh's great work which he did.

8 Therefore you shall keep the entire commandment which I command you today, that you may be strong, and go in and possess the land where you are going over to possess it, **9** and that you may prolong your days in the land which Yahweh swore to your fathers to give to them and to their offspring, a land flowing with milk and honey. **10** For the land where you go in to possess isn't like the land of Egypt, from where you came out, where you sowed your seed and watered it with your foot, as a garden of herbs; **11** but the land where you go over to possess it is a land of hills and valleys which drinks water from the rain of the sky, **12** a land which Yahweh your God cares for. **Yahweh your God's eyes are always on it, from the beginning of the year even to the end of the year**.

2Cor 5:20 **We are therefore ambassadors** on behalf of Christ, **as though God were entreating by us**: we beg you on behalf of Christ, be reconciled to God.

NOTE: Deuteronomy 11:8 of bringing in a strong way, the message of God's goodness and righteousness to the land that they are going to possess. Paul sees this as a picture of being ambassadors on behalf of Christ. Deut.11:12 is a well-known verse that shows God's powerful involvement in the physical land of Israel. Paul echoes this in the idea that God is equally interested in our spiritual ambassadorship of Christ everywhere He might send us.

De 11:13 It shall happen, if you shall listen diligently to my commandments which I command you today, to love Yahweh your God, and to serve him with all your heart and with all your soul, **14** that I will give the rain for your land in its season—the early rain and the latter rain—that you may gather in your grain, your new wine, and your oil. **15** I will give grass in your fields for your livestock, and you shall eat and be full. **16** Be careful, lest your heart be deceived, and you turn away to serve other gods and worship them; **17** and Yahweh's anger be kindled against you, and he shut up the sky so that there is no rain, and the land doesn't yield its fruit; and you perish quickly from off the good land which Yahweh gives you.

18 Therefore you shall lay up these words of mine in your heart and in your soul. You shall bind them for a sign on your hand, and they shall be for frontlets between your eyes. **19** You shall teach them to your children, talking of them when you sit in your house, when you walk by the way, when you lie down, and when you rise up. **20** You shall write them on the door posts of your house and on your gates; **21** that your days and your children's days may be multiplied in the land which Yahweh swore to your fathers to give them, as the days of the heavens above the earth. **22 For if you shall diligently keep all these commandments which I command you—to do them, to love Yahweh your God, to walk in all his ways, and to cling to him—23** then Yahweh will drive out all these nations from before you, and you shall dispossess nations greater and mightier than yourselves. **24** Every place whereon the sole of your foot treads shall be yours: from the wilderness and Lebanon, from the river, the river Euphrates, even to the western sea shall be your border. **25** No man will be able to stand before you. Yahweh your God will lay the fear of you and the dread of you on all the land that you tread on, as he has spoken to you.

2**Cor 5:20** We are therefore ambassadors on behalf of Christ, as though God were entreating by us: we beg you on behalf of Christ, **be reconciled to God**.

NOTE: [Eikev ends.] We do not interpret this echo as meaning to imply that reconciliation to God is based on works. However, our repentance from dead works and our walking in faith in God is evidenced by walking in God's ways (James 2:26). Paul knows that Israel's fullness of reconciliation will be accompanied by a diligent keeping of commandments (Deuteronomy 30:8), and so he begs us to focus on that level of comprehensive, conclusive reconciliation ourselves.

Deuteronomy 11:26	2 Cor. 5:21

De 11:26 Behold, I set before you today a blessing and a curse: **27 the blessing, if you listen to the commandments** of Yahweh your God, which I command you today; **28** and **the curse, if you do not listen to the commandments** of Yahweh your God, but turn away from the way which I command you today, to go after **other gods** which you have not known.

29 It shall happen, **when** Yahweh your God brings you into the land that you go to possess, that you shall set the blessing on Mount Gerizim, and the curse on Mount Ebal. **30** Aren't they **beyond the Jordan, behind the way of the going down of the sun**, in the land of the Canaanites who dwell in the Arabah near Gilgal, beside the oaks of Moreh? **31** For you are to pass over the Jordan to go in to possess the land which Yahweh your God gives you, and you shall possess it and dwell in it. **32** You shall observe to do all the statutes and the ordinances **which I set before you today**.

2Cor 5:21 For him **who knew no sin** he **made to be sin on our behalf**, so that in him we might become the righteousness of God.

2 Corinthians 6

6:1 Working together, we entreat also that you do not receive the grace of God in **vain**, **2** for he says, "**At an acceptable time** I listened to you. **In a day of salvation** I helped you." Behold, now is the acceptable time. Behold, **now is the day of salvation**.

NOTE: [Re'eh.] The blessings and curses at Mount Gerizim and Mount Ebal were all spoken in a single event (day). The "going down of the sun" alludes to a new day about to begin.

Deuteronomy 12

2 Cor. 6:3

De 12:1 These are the statutes and the ordinances which you shall observe to do in the land which Yahweh, the God of your fathers, has given you to possess all the days that you live on the earth. **2** You shall surely destroy all the places in which the nations that you shall possess served their gods: on the **high mountains, and on the hills**, and under every green tree. **3** You shall break down their altars, dash their pillars in pieces, and burn their Asherah poles with fire. You shall cut down the engraved images of their gods. You shall destroy their name out of that place. **4** You shall not do so to Yahweh your God. **5** But to the place which Yahweh your God shall choose out of all your tribes, to put his name there, you shall seek his habitation, and you shall come there. **6** You shall bring your burnt offerings, your sacrifices, your tithes, the wave offering of your hand, your vows, your freewill offerings, and the firstborn of your herd and of your flock there. **7** There you shall eat before Yahweh your God, and you shall rejoice in all that you put your hand to, you and your households, in which Yahweh your God has blessed you.

2**Cor 6:3** giving **no occasion of stumbling** in anything, that our service may not be blamed, **4** but in everything commending ourselves as servants of God: in great endurance, in afflictions, in hardships,

in distresses, **5** in beatings, in imprisonments,

in riots, in labors, in watchings,

in fastings, **6** in pureness, in knowledge,

in perseverance, in kindness, in the Holy Spirit,

in sincere love, **7** in the word of truth, in the power of God, by the armor of righteousness on the right hand and on the left.

NOTE: Paul now writes in his 2 Corinthians Ch. 6 a series of lists, that echo corresponding lists in Deuteronomy Ch. 12.

NOTE: The first three kinds of offerings are echoed by nine descriptions of bearing up under difficulty:

Burnt Offerings: endurance, afflictions, hardships

Sacrifices: distresses, beatings, imprisonment

Tithes: riots, labors, watchings (sleepless nights)

And then the last three kinds of offerings are echoed by nine descriptions of redemptive responses:

Wave offering: fastings, pureness, knowledge

Vows: perseverance, kindness, in the Holy Spirit

Freewill offerings: sincere love, word of truth, in the power of God

De 12:8 You shall not do all the things that we do here today, every man whatever is right in his own eyes; **9** for you haven't yet come to the rest and to the inheritance which Yahweh your God gives you. **10** But when you go over the Jordan and dwell in the land which Yahweh your God causes you to inherit, and he gives you rest from all your enemies around you, so that you dwell in safety, **11** then it shall happen that to the place which Yahweh your God shall choose, to cause his name to dwell there, there you shall bring all that I command you: your burnt offerings, your sacrifices, your tithes, the wave offering of your hand, and all your choice vows which you vow to Yahweh. **12** You shall rejoice before Yahweh your God—you, and your sons, your daughters, your male servants, your female servants, and the Levite who is within your gates, because he has no portion nor inheritance with you.

13 Be careful that you don't offer your burnt offerings in every place that you see; **14** but in the place which Yahweh chooses in one of your tribes, there you shall offer your burnt offerings, and there you shall do all that I command you.

2Cor **6:7** in the word of truth, in the power of God, by the armor of righteousness on the right hand and on the left,

8 by glory and dishonor,

by evil report and good report, as deceivers and yet true.

NOTE: The seven parts of a full household coming together in rejoicing, seem to be echoed by seven "by's." Each "by" seems to indicate a mysterious way in which God's way relates to the work of his children. By their *righteousness*, by their position on his *right* and *left* hand, by their *glory* and *dishonor* and by whether the report brought to him is a report of *good* (in the world) or *evil*.

De 12:15 Yet you may kill and eat meat within all your gates, after all the desire of your soul, according to the blessing of Yahweh your God which he has given you. The unclean and the clean may eat of it, as of the gazelle and the deer. **16** Only you shall not eat the blood. You shall pour it out on the earth like water. **17** You may not eat within your gates the tithe of your grain, or of your new wine, or of your oil, or the firstborn of your herd or of your flock, nor any of your vows which you vow, nor your freewill offerings, nor the wave offering of your hand; **18** but you shall eat them before Yahweh your God in the place which Yahweh your God shall choose—you, your son, your daughter, your male servant, your female servant, and the Levite who is within your gates. You shall rejoice before Yahweh your God in all that you put your hand to. **19** Be careful that you don't forsake the Levite as long as you live in your land.

2Cor **6:8** by glory and dishonor, by evil report and good report, as deceivers and

yet true, **9** as unknown and

yet well known, as dying and behold—we live, as punished and

not killed, **10** as sorrowful

yet always rejoicing, as poor

yet making many rich, as having nothing and

yet possessing all things.

NOTE: The seven parts of a full household coming together at the Temple, are now echoed by seven "yet's." that are just as mysterious as the seven preceding "by's" in the prior section. They are: *true, well known,* we *live, not killed, rejoicing, making many rich, possessing.*

De 12:20 When Yahweh your God enlarges your border, as he has promised you, and **you say, "I want to eat meat," because your soul desires to eat meat**, you may eat meat after all the desire of your soul. **21** If the place which Yahweh your God shall choose to put his name is too far from you, then you shall kill of your herd and of your flock, which Yahweh has given you, as I have commanded you; **and you may eat within your gates, after all the desire of your soul**. **22** Even as the gazelle and as the deer is eaten, so you shall eat of it. The unclean and the clean may eat of it alike. **23** Only be sure that you don't eat the blood; for the blood is the life, and you shall not eat the life with the meat. **24** You shall not eat it. You shall pour it out on the earth like water. **25** You shall not eat it, that it may go well with you and with your children after you, when you do that which is right in Yahweh's eyes. **26** Only your holy things which you have, and your vows, you shall take and go to the place which Yahweh shall choose. **27** You shall offer your burnt offerings, the meat and the blood, on the altar of Yahweh your God. The blood of your sacrifices shall be poured out on the altar of Yahweh your God; and you shall eat the meat.

2Cor 6:11

Our mouth is open to you, Corinthians. Our heart is enlarged.

12 **You are not restricted by us**, but you are restricted by your own affections.

NOTE: Paul turns the desire to eat, which is always through the mouth, and plays it backwards. Are their mouths open to eat what is offered by the Corinthians, or is their mouth open to speak the words of truth? Both are possible. The phrase in Deuteronomy 12:21, "after all the desire of your soul" speaks loudly of free will. Paul echoes this by emphasizing their freedom to choose.

De 12:28 Observe and hear all these words which I command you, **that it may go well with you and with your children** after you forever, when you do that which is good and right in the eyes of Yahweh your God.

29 When Yahweh your God cuts off the nations from before you, where you are going in to dispossess them, and you dispossess them, and dwell in their land, **30** be careful that you are not ensnared to follow them after they are destroyed from before you, and that you not inquire after their gods, saying, "How do these nations serve their gods? I will do likewise." **31** You shall not do so to Yahweh your God; for every abomination to Yahweh, which he hates, they have done to their gods; for they even burn their sons and their daughters in the fire to their gods.

32 Whatever thing I command you, that you shall observe to do. You shall not add to it, nor take away from it.

2Cor 6:13 Now in return—**I speak as to my children**— you also open your affections.

Deuteronomy 13 | 2 Cor. 6:14

De 13:1 If a prophet or a dreamer of dreams arises among you, and he gives you a sign or a wonder, **2** and the sign or the wonder comes to pass, of which **he spoke to you, saying, "Let us go after other gods"** (which you have not known) "and let us serve them," **3** you shall not listen to the words of that prophet, or to that dreamer of dreams; for Yahweh your God is testing you, to know whether you love Yahweh your God with all your heart and with all your soul. **4** You shall walk after Yahweh your God, fear him, keep his commandments, and obey his voice. You shall serve him, and cling to him. **5** That prophet, or that dreamer of dreams, shall be put to death, because he has spoken rebellion against Yahweh your God, who brought you out of the land of Egypt and redeemed you out of the house of bondage, to draw you aside out of the way which Yahweh your God commanded you to walk in. So you shall remove the evil from among you.

6 If your brother, the son of your mother, or your son, or your daughter, or the wife of your bosom, or your friend who is as your own soul, entices you secretly, saying, **"Let us go and serve other gods"** (which you have not known, you, nor your fathers; **7** of **the gods of the peoples who are around you, near to you, or far off from you, from the one end of the earth even to the other end of the earth)**, **8 you shall not consent to him, nor listen to him**; neither shall your eye pity him, neither shall you spare, neither shall you conceal him; **9** but you shall surely kill him. Your hand shall be first on him to put him to death, and afterwards the hand of all the people. **10** You shall stone him to death with stones, because he has sought to draw you away from Yahweh your God, who brought you out of the land of Egypt, out of the house of bondage. **11** All Israel shall hear, and fear, and shall not do any more such wickedness as this among you.

2Cor 6:14

Don't be unequally yoked with unbelievers, for **what fellowship do righteousness and iniquity have**?

Or **what fellowship does light have with darkness?** 15 **What agreement does Christ have with Belial?** Or **what portion does a believer have with an unbeliever?**

De 13:12 If you shall hear tell concerning one of your cities, which Yahweh your God gives you to dwell there, saying, **13** "Certain base fellows have gone out from among you and have drawn away the inhabitants of their city, saying, 'Let's go and serve other gods,' which you have not known," **14** then you shall inquire, make search, and ask diligently. Behold, if it is true, and the thing certain, that such abomination was done among you, **15 you shall surely strike the inhabitants of that city with the edge of the sword, destroying it utterly**, with all that is therein and its livestock, with the edge of the sword. **16** You shall gather all its spoil into the middle of its street, and shall **burn with fire the city, with all its spoil, every bit, to Yahweh your God. It shall be a heap forever. It shall not be built again**. **17** Nothing of the devoted thing shall cling to your hand, that Yahweh may turn from the fierceness of his anger and show you mercy, and **have compassion on you** and multiply you, as he has sworn to your fathers, **18** when you listen to Yahweh your God's voice, to keep all his commandments which I command you today, to do that which is right in Yahweh your God's eyes.

2Cor 6:16 **What agreement does a temple of God have with idols? For you are a temple of the living God**. Even as God said, "I will dwell in them and walk in them. I will be their God and they will be my people." **17** Therefore, "'**Come out from among them, and be separate,'** **says the Lord.**

'Touch no unclean thing.

I will receive you.'

NOTE: Paul's refence to the temple of God in 2 Corinthians 6:16 may possibly be related to the fact that one chapter earlier in Deuteronomy 12:18, God mentions gathering at "the place where my name shall dwell."

Deuteronomy 14   2 Corinthians 6:18

De 14:1 You are the children of Yahweh your God. You shall not cut yourselves, nor make any baldness between your eyes for the dead.

2Cor 6:18 "I will be to you a Father. **You will be to me sons and daughters," says the Lord Almighty**.

NOTE: Paul's often takes a thought in one text, and then expands it by quoting from better known verses elsewhere. 2 Corinthians 6:18 seems combine multiple verses together into one. Why then did Paul not quote Deuteronomy 14:1 directly? Possibly because it might have led to questions about the meaning of the accompanying prohibitions to an audience not familiar with the intricacies of Jewish law.

Deuteronomy 14:2   2 Cor. 7

De 14:2 For you are a holy people to Yahweh your God, and **Yahweh has chosen you to be a people for his own possession**, above all peoples who are on the face of the earth.

3 You shall not eat any abominable thing. **4** These are the animals which you may eat: the ox, the sheep, the goat, **5** the deer, the gazelle, the roebuck, the wild goat, the ibex, the antelope, and the chamois. **6** Every animal that parts the hoof, and has the hoof split in two and chews the cud, among the animals, that may you eat. **7** Nevertheless these you shall not eat of them that chew the cud, or of those who have the hoof split: the camel, the hare, and the rabbit. Because they chew the cud but don't part the hoof, they are <u>unclean</u> to you. **8** The pig, because it has a split hoof but doesn't chew the cud, is <u>unclean</u> to you. You shall not eat their meat or touch their carcasses.

9 These you may eat of all that are in the waters: whatever has fins and scales may you eat; **10** and whatever doesn't have fins and scales you shall not eat. It is <u>unclean</u> to you.

11 All clean birds you may eat. **12** But these are they of which you shall not eat: the eagle, the vulture, the osprey, **13** the red kite, the falcon, the kite after its kind, **14** every raven after its kind, **15** the ostrich, the owl, the seagull, the hawk after its kind, **16** the little owl, the great owl, the horned owl, **17** the pelican, the vulture, the cormorant, **18** the stork, the heron after its kind, the hoopoe, and the bat. **19** All winged creeping things are <u>unclean</u> to you. They shall not be eaten. **20** Of all clean birds you may eat.

21 You shall not eat of anything that dies of itself. You may give it to the foreigner living among you who is within your gates, that he may eat it, or you may sell it to a foreigner; for **you are a holy people to Yahweh your God**. You shall not boil a young goat in its mother's milk.

2Cor 7:1 Having therefore **these promises**, beloved, **let's cleanse ourselves** from <u>all defilement</u> of flesh and spirit, **perfecting holiness in the fear of God**.

NOTE: Paul's avoids direct references to unclean eating, but his use of both "flesh and spirit" leaves open the interpretation of clean eating, without forcing it on his readers. In any event, one of the primary meanings of the Hebrew word *tame* translated here as "unclean" is "defiled," and one of the alternate meanings of the underlying Greek word *molusmos* translated here as "defilement," is "filthiness." The last sentence of Deut.14:21 "You shall not boil a young goat in its mother's milk," is well-known to be the basis for separation of meat and milk in the Jewish diet. The reasoning from this specific command (repeated three times in the Torah) to the general separation of meat and milk, won't be detailed here, however it is fascinating that Paul's use of "perfecting holiness" (i.e. separation) and "fear of God" are some of the reasons used to support the reasoning of from specific to general! The editors find it fascinating that regardless of one's position on whether the complete separation of meat and milk is biblical, support for both positions may be found in Paul's echoes.

De 14:22 You shall surely tithe all the increase of your seed, that which comes out of the field year by year. **23** You shall eat before Yahweh your God, in the place which he chooses to cause his name to dwell there, the tithe of your grain, of your new wine, and of your oil, and the firstborn of your herd and of your flock; that you may learn to fear Yahweh your God always. **24** If the way is too long for you, so that you are not able to carry it because the place which Yahweh your God shall choose to set his name there is too far from you, when Yahweh your God blesses you, **25** then you shall turn it into money, bind up the money in your hand, and shall go to the place which Yahweh your God shall choose. **26** You shall trade the money for whatever your soul desires: for cattle, or for sheep, or for wine, or for strong drink, or for whatever your soul asks of you; and you shall eat there before Yahweh your God, and **you shall rejoice**, you and your household. **27 You shall not forsake the Levite who is within your gates, for he has no portion nor inheritance with you**.

28 At the end of every three years you shall bring all the tithe of your increase in the same year, and shall store it within your gates. **29** The Levite, because he has no portion nor inheritance with you, the foreigner living among you, the fatherless, and the widow who are within your gates shall come, and shall eat and be satisfied; that Yahweh your God may bless you in all the work of your hand which you do.

2Cor 7:2 Open your hearts to us. We wronged no one. We corrupted no one. We took advantage of no one. **3** I say this not to condemn you, for I have said before that you are in our hearts to die together and live together. **4** Great is my boldness of speech toward you. Great is my boasting on your behalf. I am filled with comfort. **I overflow with joy** in all our affliction.

NOTE: Many echoes in this pairing are possible, but most of them are not in strict order. In fact the only two echoes highlighted above are **out of order**. Another possible echo is Paul's parallelism of the three "We ___ no one" statements in 2 Corinthians 7:2 that might echo the phase "at the end of three years," in Deuteronomy14:28.

Deuteronomy 15   2 Cor. 7:5

De 15:1 At the end of every seven years, **you shall cancel debts**.
2 This is the way it shall be done: every creditor shall release that
which he has lent to his neighbor. He shall not require it of his
neighbor and his brother, because Yahweh's release has been
proclaimed. **3** Of a foreigner you may require it; but whatever of yours
is with your brother, your hand shall release. **4** However there will be
no poor with you (for Yahweh will surely bless you in the land which
Yahweh your God gives you for an inheritance to possess), **5** if only
you diligently listen to Yahweh your God's voice, to observe to do all
this commandment which I command you today. **6** For Yahweh your
God will bless you, as he promised you. You will lend to many
nations, but you will not borrow. You will rule over many nations, but
they will not rule over you.

7 If a poor man, one of your brothers, is with you within any of your
gates in your land which Yahweh your God gives you, you shall not
harden your heart, nor shut your hand from your poor brother; **8** but
you shall surely open your hand to him, and shall surely lend him
sufficient for his need in that which he lacks. **9** Beware that there not
be a wicked thought in your heart, saying, "The seventh year, the
year of release, is at hand," and your eye be evil against your poor
brother and you give him nothing; and he cry to Yahweh against you,
and it be sin to you. **10** You shall surely give, and your heart shall not
be grieved when you give to him, because for this thing Yahweh your
God will bless you in all your work and in all that you put your hand
to. **11** For the poor will never cease out of the land. **Therefore I
command you to surely open your hand to your brother, to your
needy, and to your poor, in your land**.

12 If your brother, a Hebrew man, or a Hebrew woman, is sold to you
and serves you six years, then in the seventh year you shall let him
go free from you. **13** When you let him go free from you, you shall not
let him go empty. **14** You shall furnish him liberally out of your flock,
out of your threshing floor, and out of your wine press. As Yahweh
your God has blessed you, you shall give to him.

2**Cor 7:5** For even
when we had come
into Macedonia,
**our flesh had no
relief**, but we were
afflicted on every
side. Fightings
were outside. Fear
was inside. **6**
Nevertheless, **he
who comforts the
lowly**, God,
comforted us by the
coming of Titus.

NOTE: In Deuteronomy 15:11, the second use of the word poor, is the Hebrew word *ani*, which can
also be translated *humble* or *lowly*.

De 15:15 You shall remember that you were a slave in the land of Egypt, and Yahweh your God redeemed you. Therefore I command you this thing today. **16** It shall be, if he tells you, "I will not go out from you," **because he loves you and your house, because he is well with you, 17** then you shall take an awl, and thrust it through his ear to the door, and he shall be your servant forever. Also to your female servant you shall do likewise.

18 It shall not seem hard to you when you let him go free from you; for he has been worth a double hired hand to you in serving you six years. Yahweh your God will bless you in all that you do.

19 You shall dedicate all the firstborn males that are born of your herd and of your flock to Yahweh your God. You shall do no work with the firstborn of your herd, nor shear the firstborn of your flock. **20** You shall eat it before Yahweh your God year by year in the place which Yahweh shall choose, you and your household. **21** If it has any defect—is lame or blind, or has any defect whatever, you shall not sacrifice it to Yahweh your God. **22** You shall eat it within your gates. The unclean and the clean shall eat it alike, as the gazelle and as the deer. **23** Only you shall not eat its blood. You shall pour it out on the ground like water.

2Cor 7:7 and not by his coming only, but also by the comfort with which he was comforted in you, while he told us of your longing, your mourning, and your zeal for me, so that I rejoiced still more. **8** For though I grieved you with my letter, I do not regret it, though I did regret it. For I see that my letter made you grieve, though just for a while. **9** I now rejoice, not that you were grieved, but that you were grieved to repentance. For you were grieved in a godly way, that you might suffer loss by us in nothing. **10** For godly sorrow produces repentance to salvation, which brings no regret. But the sorrow of the world produces death. **11** For behold, this same thing, that you were grieved in a godly way, what earnest care it worked in you. Yes, what defense, indignation, fear, longing, zeal, and vengeance! In everything you demonstrated yourselves to be pure in this matter. **12** So although I wrote to you, I wrote not for his cause that did the wrong, nor for his cause that suffered the wrong, but that your earnest care for us might be revealed in you in the sight of God. **13** Therefore we have been comforted.

In our comfort we rejoiced the more exceedingly for the joy of Titus, because his spirit has been refreshed by you all. **14** For if in anything I have boasted to him on your behalf, I was not disappointed. But as we spoke all things to you in truth, so our glorying also which I made before Titus was found to be truth. **15 His affection is more abundantly toward you**, while he remembers all of your obedience, how with fear and trembling you received him. **16** I rejoice that in everything I am confident concerning you.

NOTE: Titus's affection has been turned towards the Corinthians.

Deuteronomy 16	2 Cor. 8

De 16:1 Observe the month of Abib, and keep the Passover to Yahweh your God; for in the month of Abib Yahweh your **God brought you out of Egypt** by night. **2** You shall sacrifice the Passover to Yahweh your God, of the flock and the herd, in the place which Yahweh shall choose to cause his name to dwell there. **3** You shall eat no leavened bread with it. You shall eat unleavened bread with it seven days, even the bread of affliction (for you came out of the land of Egypt in haste) that you may remember the day when you came out of the land of Egypt all the days of your life. **4** No yeast shall be seen with you in all your borders seven days; neither shall any of the meat, which you sacrifice the first day at evening, remain all night until the morning. **5** You may not sacrifice the Passover within any of your gates which Yahweh your God gives you; **6** but at the place which Yahweh your God shall choose to cause his name to dwell in, there you shall sacrifice the Passover at evening, at the going down of the sun, at the season that you came out of Egypt. **7** You shall roast and eat it in the place which Yahweh your God chooses. In the morning you shall return to your tents. **8** Six days you shall eat unleavened bread. On the seventh day shall be a solemn assembly to Yahweh your God. You shall do no work.

2Cor **8:1** Moreover, brothers, we make known to you the grace of God which has been given in the churches of Macedonia, **2 how in much proof of affliction, the abundance of their joy and their deep poverty abounded to the riches of their generosity**. **3** For according to their power, I testify, yes and beyond their power, they gave of their own accord, **4** begging us with much entreaty to receive this grace and the fellowship in the service to the saints. **5** This was not as we had expected, but first they gave their own selves to the Lord, and to us through the will of God. **6** So we urged Titus, that as he had made a beginning before, so he would also complete in you this grace.

NOTE: The Children of Israel came out of Egypt with many riches, given to them willingly by the Egyptians (Psalm 105:37). In Macedonia their generosity abounded even though they had little material wealth. Paul was astounded by the example they set for other assemblies.

De 16:9 You shall count for yourselves seven weeks. From the time you begin to put the sickle to the standing grain you shall begin to count seven weeks. **10** You shall keep the feast of weeks to Yahweh your God with a tribute of **a free will offering of your hand**, which you shall give **according to how Yahweh your God blesses you**. **11** You shall rejoice before Yahweh your God—you, your son, your daughter, your male servant, your female servant, the Levite who is within your gates, the foreigner, the fatherless, and the widow who are among you—in the place which Yahweh your God shall choose to cause his name to dwell there. **12** You shall remember that you were a slave in Egypt. You shall observe and do these statutes.

13 You shall keep the feast of booths seven days, after that you have gathered in from your threshing floor and from your wine press. **14** You shall rejoice in your feast, you, your son, your daughter, your male servant, your female servant, the Levite, the foreigner, the fatherless, and the widow who are within your gates. **15** You shall keep a feast to Yahweh your God seven days in the place which Yahweh chooses, because Yahweh your God will bless you in all your increase and in all the work of your hands, and you shall be altogether joyful.

16 Three times **in a year** all of your males shall appear before Yahweh your God in the place which he chooses: in the feast of unleavened bread, in the feast of weeks, and in the feast of booths. They shall not appear before Yahweh empty. **17** <u>**Every man shall give as he is able, according to Yahweh your God's blessing which he has given you**</u>.

2Cor 8:7 But as you abound in everything—in faith, utterance, knowledge, all earnestness, and in your love to us—see that you also abound in this grace. **8 I speak not by way of commandment**, but as proving through the earnestness of others the sincerity also of your love. **9** For you know the grace of our Lord Jesus Christ, that <u>**though he was rich, yet for your sakes he became poor, that you through his poverty might become rich**</u>. **10** I give a judgment in this: for this is expedient for **you who were the first to start a year ago**, not only to do, but also to be willing. **11** But now complete the doing also, that as there was the readiness to be willing, so there may be the completion also out of your ability. **12** For if the readiness is there, it is acceptable <u>**according to what you have**</u>, not according to what you don't have. **13** For this is not that others may be eased and you distressed, **14** but for equality. Your abundance at this present time supplies their lack, that their abundance also may become a supply for your lack, that there may be equality. **15** As it is written, "He who gathered much had nothing left over, and he who gathered little had no lack."

NOTE: [Re'eh ends.] In Deuteronomy 16:16, the phrase "They shall not appear before Yahweh empty," summarizes Paul's exhortation. Paul has already summarized the great fulfillment of God's intent when he wrote in the previous pairing, "For according to their power, I testify, yes and beyond their power, they gave," (2 Corinthians 8:3).

De 16:18 You shall **make** judges and officers in all your gates, which Yahweh your God gives you, according to your tribes; and they shall **judge** the people with righteous judgment. **19** You shall not pervert justice. **You shall not show partiality**. You shall not take a **bribe**, for a bribe blinds the eyes of the wise and perverts the words of the righteous. **20 You shall follow that which is altogether just**, that you may live and inherit the land which Yahweh your God gives you.

21 You shall **not plant for yourselves an Asherah of any kind of tree** beside the altar of Yahweh your God, which you shall make for yourselves.

2Cor 8:16 But thanks be to God, who puts the same earnest care for you into the heart of Titus. **17** For he accepted our exhortation, but being himself very earnest, he went out to you of his own accord. **18** We have sent together with him the brother whose praise in the Good News is known through all the churches. **19** Not only so, but he was also **appointed** by the churches to travel with us in this grace, which is **served** by us to the glory of the Lord himself, and to show our readiness. **20 We are avoiding this, that any man should blame us** concerning this **abundance** which is **administered by us**. **21 Having regard for honorable things, not only in the sight of the Lord, but also in the sight of men**. **22** We have sent with them our brother, whom we have many times proved earnest in many things, but now much more earnest, by reason of the great confidence which he has in you. **23** As for **Titus, he is my partner and fellow worker** for you. As for our brothers, they are the messengers of the churches, the glory of Christ.

NOTE: [Shoftim.] In Deuteronomy 16:18, *make* is often translated as *appointed*. In 2 Corinthians 8:19, *served* is often translated as *administered*. The echo for Titus in 2 Cor. 8:23 is reasoned as follows: Titus is a proven, earnest partner and fellow worker of Paul. On the other hand, an Asherah tree that is foreign and opposed to the work performed at the "altar," yet is planted "beside" it. Paul is not only asking the Corinthians to accept Titus, but by implication, he is giving them a standard by which to judge future workers who might be invited (planted) into the midst of the assembly.

Deuteronomy 17

2 Corinthians 8:24

De 17:1 You shall not sacrifice to Yahweh your God an ox or a sheep in which is a defect or anything evil; for that is an abomination to Yahweh your God.

2Cor 8:24 Therefore show the proof of your love to them before the churches, and of our boasting on your behalf.

Deuteronomy 17:2

2 Corinthians 9

De 17:2 If there is found among you, within any of **your gates which Yahweh your God gives you**, a man or woman who does that which is evil in Yahweh your God's sight in transgressing his covenant, **3** and has gone and **served** other gods and worshiped them, or the sun, or the moon, or any of the army of the sky, which I have not commanded, **4** and it is told you, and you have heard of it, then you shall inquire *diligently*. Behold, if it is true, and the thing certain, that such abomination is done in Israel, **5** then you shall **bring out** that man or that woman who has done this evil thing to your gates, even that same man or woman; and you shall stone them to death with stones.

2Cor 9:1 It is indeed unnecessary **for me to write to you** concerning the **service** to the saints, **2** for I know your *readiness*, of which I **boast** on your behalf to the Macedonians, that Achaia has been prepared for a year past. Your zeal has stirred up very many of them.

NOTE: The gates of a city often refers to its oversight by its leaders. Paul recognizes that the leadership in the Corinthian assembly is already performing well in this area of oversight.

De 17:6 At the mouth of two witnesses, or three witnesses, he who is to die shall be put to death. At the mouth of one witness he shall not be put to death. **7** The hand of the witnesses shall be first on him to put him to death, and afterward the hand of all the people. So you shall remove the evil from among you.

8 If there arises a matter too hard for you in judgment, between blood and blood, between plea and plea, or between stroke and stroke, being matters of controversy within your gates, then you shall arise, and go up to the place which Yahweh your God chooses. **9 You shall come** to the priests who are Levites and to the judge who shall be in those days. You shall **inquire**, and they shall show you the sentence of judgment. **10** You shall do according to the tenor of the sentence which they shall show you from that place which Yahweh chooses. You shall observe to do according to all that they shall teach you. **11** According to the tenor of the law which they shall teach you, and according to the judgment which they shall tell you, you shall do. You shall not turn away from the sentence which they shall show you, to the right hand, nor to the left. **12** The man who does presumptuously in not listening to the priest who stands to minister there before Yahweh your God, or to the judge, even that man shall die. You shall put away the evil from Israel. **13** All the people shall hear and fear, and do no more presumptuously.

2Cor 9:3 But **I have sent the brothers** that our boasting on your behalf may not be in vain in this respect, that, as I said, you may be prepared, **4** lest by any means, **if anyone from Macedonia comes** with me and **finds** you unprepared, we (to say nothing of you) would be disappointed in this confident boasting.

NOTE: In 2 Corinthians 9:3, "the brothers" refers to the two brothers mentioned in 2 Cor. 8:16-18.

De 17:14 When you have come to the land which Yahweh your God gives you, and possess it, and dwell in it, and say, "I will set a king over me, like all the nations that are around me," **15** you shall surely set him king over yourselves whom Yahweh your God chooses. You shall set as king over you one from **among your brothers**. You may not put a foreigner over you, who is not your brother. **16** Only **he shall not multiply horses to himself**, nor cause the people to return to Egypt, to the end that he may multiply horses; because Yahweh has said to you, "You shall not go back that way again." **17** He shall not multiply wives to himself, that his heart not turn away. **He shall not greatly multiply to himself silver and gold**.

2**Cor 9:5** I thought it necessary therefore to **entreat the brothers** that they would go before to you and **arrange ahead of time the generous gift** that you promised before, that the same might be ready **as a matter of generosity, and not of greediness**.

NOTE: In Deuteronomy 17:16, the king is to not to multiply horses to *himself*, but by implication there was no prohibition against the king multiplying horses to be given to *others*!

De 17:18 It shall be, when he sits on the throne of his kingdom, that he shall **write** himself a copy of this law in a book, out of that which is before the priests the Levites. **19** It shall be with him, and he shall read from it all the days of his life, that he may learn to fear Yahweh his God, to keep all the words of this law and these statutes, to do them; **20** that his **heart** not be lifted up above his brothers, and that he not turn away from the commandment, to the right hand, or to the left, to the end that he may prolong his days in his kingdom, he and his children, in the middle of Israel.

2**Cor 9:6** Remember this: he who sows sparingly will also reap sparingly.

He who **sows bountifully** will also reap bountifully. **7** Let each man give according as he has determined in his **heart**, not grudgingly or under compulsion, for God loves a cheerful giver.

NOTE: The first echo proposed here is based on the idea that the "writing" of the law is a spiritual discipline that is in fact "sowing" the Word of God into one's own life. In the second echo, while the "reading" of what is written may also be viewed as another spiritual discipline, (i.e. further sowing), perhaps Paul sees a form of bountiful reaping from it, as well, perhaps in a phrase in Deuteronomy 17:20, "to the end that he may prolong his days in his kingdom."

Deuteronomy 18

2 Corinthians 9:8

De 18:1 The priests the Levites, all the tribe of Levi, shall have no portion nor inheritance with Israel. They shall eat the offerings of Yahweh made by fire and his portion. **2** They shall have no inheritance among their brothers. **Yahweh is their inheritance**, as he has spoken to them.

3 This shall be the priests' due from the people, from those who offer a sacrifice, whether it be ox or sheep, **that they shall give to the priest** the shoulder, the two cheeks, and the inner parts. **4** You shall give him **the first fruits** of your grain, of your new wine, and of your oil, and the first of the fleece of your sheep. **5** For Yahweh your God has chosen him out of all your tribes to stand to minister in Yahweh's name, him and his sons forever.

6 If a Levite comes from any of your gates out of all Israel where he lives, and comes with all the desire of his soul to the place which Yahweh shall choose, **7** then **he shall minister in the name of Yahweh his God**, as all **his brothers the Levites** do, who stand there before Yahweh. **8** They shall have like portions to eat, in addition to that which comes from the sale of his patrimony.

2Cor 9:8 **And God is able to make all grace abound to you**, that you, always having all sufficiency in everything, may abound to every good work. **9** As it is written, "He has scattered abroad. **He has given to the poor**. His righteousness remains forever." **10** Now may he who supplies seed to the sower and bread for food, supply and multiply your seed for sowing, and **increase the fruits** of your righteousness, **11** you being enriched in everything to all generosity, which produces thanksgiving to God through us. **12 For this service of giving that you perform** not only makes up for lack **among the saints**, but abounds also through much giving of thanks to God,

NOTE: In Deuteronomy 18:6, the echo of "Levite" with "generosity" is reminds us of Zacharias (Luke 1:8), who considered it a great honor to have the privilege of serving at the temple in Jerusalem. Zacharias was surprised that in the midst of that service, a deep desire of his heart had been granted, even though he did not understand it at first. Paul's language in this echo honors all believers who generously give and serve, seeing in it a great privilege and part of a long-term process of growth and thanksgiving. This is one of many examples in the Echoes Bible where Paul sees something physically beautiful in the Torah, and reframes it into a spiritual gift to be given to the entire Gentile world, in a form that they (we) can understand and receive. Is it any wonder that Paul's writings were ultimately given the high honor of forming so much of the New Testament?

NOTE: A few additional echoes are not in sequential order, perhaps due to the quotation, but may also apply. The word *forever* in 2 Corinthians 9:9 echoes *forever* in Deut. 18:5. The words *seed* or *bread* in 2 Cor. 9:10 may echo *grain* in Deut.18:4.

De 18:9 When you have come into the land which Yahweh your God gives you, you shall not learn to imitate the abominations of those nations. **10** There shall not be found with you anyone who makes his son or his daughter to pass through the fire, one who uses divination, one who tells fortunes, or an enchanter, or a sorcerer, **11** or a charmer, or someone who consults with a familiar spirit, or a wizard, or a necromancer. **12** For whoever does these things is an abomination to Yahweh. Because of these abominations, Yahweh your God drives them out from before you. **13 You shall be perfect with Yahweh your God**. **14 For these nations**, which you shall dispossess, listen to those who practice sorcery and to diviners; but as for you, Yahweh your God has not allowed you so to do.

2Cor 9:13 seeing that through the proof given by this service, they **glorify God for the obedience** of your confession to the **Good News of Christ** and for the generosity of your contribution to them and to all, **14** while they themselves also, with supplication on your behalf, yearn for you by reason of the exceeding grace of God in you. **15** Thanks be to God for his unspeakable gift!

NOTE: The theme of this pairing in Deuteronomy is that of the need to dispossess sinful nations of their sin. But the full heart of God is for those nations to hear the good news of Jesus Christ and be transformed from the kingdom of darkness to that of His own dear son." (Colossians 1:13)   By implication Paul sees "being perfect" in Deuteronomy 18:13 as including the confession of the Good News of Christ to the nations. See also the notes after Deut. 2:14, 7:12, and 20:1.

Deuteronomy 18:15	2 Corinthians 10

De 18:15 Yahweh your God will **raise up to you a prophet** from among you, **of your brothers**, **like me**. You shall listen to him. **16** This is according to all that you desired of Yahweh your God in Horeb in the day of the assembly, saying, "**Let me not hear again Yahweh my God's voice, neither let me see this great fire any more, that I not die**." **17** Yahweh said to me, "They have well said that which they have spoken. **18** I will raise them up a prophet from among their brothers, like you. **I will put my words in his mouth**, and **he shall speak to them all that I shall command him**. **19** It shall happen, that **whoever will not listen to my words which he shall speak in my name, I will require it of him**. **20** But the prophet who speaks a word presumptuously in my name, which I have not commanded him to speak, or who speaks in the name of other gods, that same prophet shall die." **21** If you say in your heart, "How shall we know the word which Yahweh has not spoken?" **22** When a prophet speaks in Yahweh's name, if the thing doesn't follow, nor happen, that is the thing which Yahweh has not spoken. The prophet has spoken it presumptuously. You shall not be afraid of him.

2Cor 10:1 Now **I Paul, myself**, entreat <u>you</u> by the **humility and gentleness of Christ**, I who in your presence am lowly among you, but being absent am bold toward you. **2** Yes, I beg you that I may not, when present, show courage with the confidence with which I intend to be bold against some, <u>who consider us to be walking according to the flesh</u>. **3** For though we walk in the flesh, we don't wage war according to the flesh; **4** for **the weapons of our warfare are not of the flesh**, but mighty before God to the throwing down of strongholds, **5** throwing down imaginations and every high thing that is exalted against the knowledge of God, and <u>**bringing every thought into captivity to the obedience of Christ**</u>, **6** and being **in readiness to avenge all disobedience when your obedience is made full**.

NOTE: This is only the second time that Paul mentions his own name in 2 Corinthians. Here, he stops short of calling himself a prophet even though his spiritual authority over the Corinthians is undisputed. Instead he only recalls within himself the desire, like Moses, to be one who is humble and gentle in his leadership, and like Moses, Paul points past himself to another greater prophet who whose humility and gentleness is beyond all of us: Christ Jesus. The echo of "I will put my words in his mouth" with "the weapons of our warfare are not of the flesh," can be view from at least two perspectives. First, praise and thanksgiving can be warfare (2 Chronicles 20:21-22). Second, when Christ returns he will defeat the enemies of God with the sword of his mouth (Revelation 19:14).

Deuteronomy 19

2 Corinthians 10:7

De 19:1 When Yahweh your God cuts off the nations whose land Yahweh your God gives you, and you succeed them and **dwell in their cities and in their houses**, **2** you shall set apart three cities for yourselves in the middle of your land, which Yahweh your God gives you to possess. **3** You shall prepare the way, and **divide the borders of your land** which Yahweh your God causes you to inherit into three parts, that every man slayer may flee there.

4 This is the case of the man slayer who shall flee there and live: whoever kills his neighbor unintentionally, and didn't hate him in time past; **5** as when a man goes into the forest with his neighbor to chop wood and his hand <u>swings the axe to cut down the tree, and the head</u> slips from the handle and hits his neighbor so that he dies—**he shall flee to one of these cities and live**. **6** Otherwise, the avenger of blood might pursue the man slayer while his heart is hot, and overtake him, because the way is long, and strike him mortally, even though he was not worthy of death, because he didn't hate him in time past. **7** Therefore I command you to set apart three cities for yourselves.

8 If Yahweh your God enlarges your border, as he has sworn to your fathers, and gives you all the land which he promised to give to your fathers; **9** if you keep all this commandment to do it, which I command you today, to love Yahweh your God, and to walk ever in his ways, then you shall add three cities more for yourselves, besides these three. **10** This is so that innocent blood not be shed in the middle of your land which Yahweh your God gives you for an inheritance, and so blood be on you.

2Cor 10:7 Do you look at things only as they appear in front of your face? If anyone trusts in himself that he is Christ's, let him consider this again with himself, **that even as he is Christ's, so we also are Christ's**. **8** For even if I boast somewhat abundantly concerning our authority, which the Lord gave for building you up and not for casting you down, I will not be ashamed, **9** that I may not seem as if I desire to terrify you by my letters.

10 For, "<u>His letters," they say, "are weighty and strong</u>, but his **bodily presence is weak**, and his speech is despised."

NOTE: The word *head* in Deuteronomy 19:5 is actually *iron*. Indeed an axe by its construction is both weighty and strong. Knowing he is echoing an axe, the editors wonder if Paul might have been smiling at the wordplay.

NOTE: The overall theme of this pairing in Deuteronomy is that after they are successful in the land, they are to add – (i.e. build) – three additional cities for the man slayer to flee. This work may seem unnecessary taking both time and expense, but God says it is important for the health of the overall community. Paul echoes this idea in 2 Corinthians 10:8 succinctly with the phrase, *building you up*.

De 19:11 But if any man hates his neighbor, lies in wait for him, rises up against him, strikes him mortally so that he dies, and he flees into one of these cities; **12** then the elders of his city shall send and bring him there, and deliver him into the hand of the avenger of blood, that he may die. **13** Your eye shall not pity him, but you shall purge the innocent blood from Israel that it may go well with you.

14 You shall not remove your neighbor's landmark, which they of old time have set, in your inheritance which you shall inherit, in the land that Yahweh your God gives you to possess.

15 One witness shall not rise up against a man for any iniquity, or for any sin that he sins. At the **mouth** of two witnesses, or at the mouth of three witnesses, shall a matter be established. **16** If an unrighteous witness rises up against any man to testify against him of **wrongdoing**, **17** then both the men, between whom the controversy is, shall stand before Yahweh, before the priests and the judges who shall be in those days; **18** and the judges shall make diligent inquisition: and behold, if the witness is a false witness, and has testified falsely against his brother, **19** then you shall do to him as he had thought to do to his brother. So you shall remove the evil from among you. **20** Those who remain shall hear, and fear, and will never again commit any such evil among you. **21** Your eyes shall not pity: life for life, eye for eye, tooth for tooth, hand for hand, foot for foot.

2Cor 10:11 Let such a person consider this, that what we are in **word** by letters when we are absent, such are we also in **deed** when we are present.

Deuteronomy 20   2 Cor. 10:12

De 20:1 When you go out to battle against your enemies, and see horses, chariots, and a **people more numerous than you**, you shall not be afraid of them; for Yahweh your God is with you, who brought you up out of the land of Egypt. **2** It shall be, when you draw near to the battle, that the priest shall approach and speak to the people, **3** and shall tell them, "Hear, Israel, you draw near today to battle against your enemies. Don't let your heart faint! Don't be afraid, nor tremble, neither be scared of them; **4** for <u>Yahweh your God is he who goes with you, to fight for you against your enemies, to save you</u>." **5** The officers shall speak to the people, saying, "What man is there who has <u>built a new house</u>, and has not dedicated it? Let him go and return to his house, lest he die in the battle, and another man dedicate it. **6** What man is there who has <u>planted a vineyard</u>, and has not used its fruit? Let him go and return to his house, lest he die in the battle, and another man use its fruit. **7** What man is there who has <u>pledged to be married to a wife</u>, and has not taken her? Let him go and return to his house, lest he die in the battle, and another man take her." **8** The officers shall speak further to the people, and they shall say, "What man is there who is <u>fearful and fainthearted</u>? Let him go and return to his house, lest his brother's heart melt as his heart." **9** It shall be, when the officers have **finished speaking to the people, that they shall appoint captains of armies at the head of the people**.

2Cor 10:12 For we are not bold to **number or compare ourselves** with some of those who commend themselves. But they themselves, measuring themselves by themselves, and comparing themselves with themselves, are without understanding. **13** But <u>**we will not boast beyond proper limits, but within the boundaries with which God appointed to us**</u>, which reach even to you. **14** <u>For we don't stretch ourselves too much</u>, as though we didn't reach to you. For we came even as far as to you with the Good News of Christ, **15** not boasting beyond proper limits in other men's labors, but having hope that **as your faith grows, we will be abundantly enlarged by you** in our sphere of influence.

NOTE: God guided Israel's armies to take ground only within the boundaries prescribed by God. Paul echoes this in 2 Corinthians 10:13. Regarding Deuteronomy 20:9, the captains of armies lead armies to capturing new ground. In the same way Paul sees that as the faith of the Corinthians grows, the ground they can take will be enlarged, which will result in a larger sphere of influence for Paul. Additionally in Deut. 20:1-4 are six references to enemies: v1 *enemies, people,* and *of them*; in v3, *enemies,* and *of them*; and in v4, *enemies.* This echoes in 2 Cor. 10:12 the six references to the Greek word *heatou*: *ourselves,* commend *themselves,* measuring *themselves* by *themselves,* comparing *themselves* with *themselves.* Deut. 20:5-8 list four different examples of people who may be excused from the battle, because in their particular situations, to engage in the battle would be truly over-extending themselves, because of their circumstances, or in the fourth case, because of fear. Paul echoes this principle this in 2 Cor.10:14 when he writes of his own team "we don't stretch ourselves too much." And in an allusion to the *battle* motif, Paul adds in verse 14 "For we came even as far as you with the Good News of Christ." Once again, he sees that winning the *battle* means bringing the Good News of Christ to far off places. See also the note after Deut. 18:9.

De 20:10 When you draw near to a city to fight against it, then **proclaim peace to it**. **11** It shall be, if it gives you answer of peace and opens to you, then it shall be that all the people who are found therein shall become forced labor to you, and shall serve you. **12** If it will make no peace with you, but will make war against you, then you shall besiege it. **13** When Yahweh your God delivers it into your hand, you shall strike every male of it with the edge of the sword; **14** but the women, the little ones, the livestock, and all that is in the city, even all its spoil, you shall take for plunder for yourself. You may use the spoil of your enemies, which Yahweh your God has given you. **15** <u>Thus you shall do to all the cities which are very far off from you</u>, which are not of the cities of these nations. **16** But of the **cities of these peoples that Yahweh your God gives you** for an inheritance, you shall save alive nothing that breathes; **17** but you shall utterly destroy them: the Hittite, the Amorite, the Canaanite, the Perizzite, the Hivite, and the Jebusite, as Yahweh your God has commanded you; **18** <u>that they not teach you to follow all their abominations</u>, which they have done for their gods; so would you sin against **Yahweh your God**.

19 When you shall besiege a city a long time, in making war against it to take it, you shall not destroy its trees by wielding an axe against them; for you may eat of them. You shall not cut them down, for is the tree of the field a man, that it should be besieged by you? **20** Only the trees that you know are not trees for food, you shall destroy and cut them down. You shall build bulwarks against the city that makes war with you, until it falls.

2Cor 10:16 yes, **we will reach even to the parts beyond you** into <u>regions where we have not preached</u>, and **not boast in another's territory** in regards to things ready to our hand. **17** But "he who **boasts**, let him **boast in the Lord**."

NOTE: The phrase *Yahweh your God* in Deuteronomy 20:18 keeps the focus of the people on their relationship to Yahweh, not just the absence of sin. Given that Paul is speaking on the topic of boasting, he transforms something that could well be sin, into something that glorifies God through relationship with God.

Deuteronomy 21   2 Cor. 10:18

De 21:1 If someone is found slain in the land which Yahweh your God gives you to possess, lying in the field, and it isn't known who has struck him, **2** then your elders and your judges shall come out, and they shall measure to the cities which are around him who is slain. **3** It shall be that the elders of the city which is nearest to the slain man shall take a heifer of the herd, which hasn't been worked with, and which has not drawn in the yoke. **4** The elders of that city shall bring the heifer down to a valley with running water, which is neither plowed nor sown, and shall break the heifer's neck there in the valley. **5** The priests the sons of Levi shall come near, for them Yahweh your God has chosen to minister to him, and to bless in Yahweh's name; and according to their word shall every controversy and every assault be decided. **6** All the elders of that city who are nearest to the slain man shall wash their hands over the heifer whose neck was broken in the valley. **7 They shall answer and say, "Our hands have not shed this blood, neither have our eyes seen it**. **8** Forgive, Yahweh, your people Israel, whom you have redeemed, and don't allow innocent blood among your people Israel." **The blood shall be forgiven them**. **9** So you shall put away the innocent blood from among you, when you shall do that which is right in Yahweh's eyes.

2Cor 10:18 For it isn't he who commends himself who is approved, _but whom the Lord commends_.

NOTE: [Shoftim ends.] In Deuteronomy 21:7, the elders cannot rightfully speak for their entire community and "commend the community" from any wrongdoing. They are restrained by God to only speak about what they have personally seen and done. But after those words, when the Lord speaks His forgiveness on the people, the gap is closed, and the matter is settled.

Deuteronomy 21:10	2 Corinthians 11

De 21:10 When you go out to battle against your enemies, and Yahweh your God delivers them into your hands and you carry them away captive, **11** and **see among the captives a beautiful woman**, and you have a **desire** to her, that you would **take her as your wife**, **12** then you shall bring her home to your house. She shall shave her head, and trim her nails. **13** <u>She shall take off the clothing of her captivity</u>, and shall remain in your house, and lament her father and her mother a full month. After that you shall go in to her and be her husband, and she shall be your wife. **14** It shall be, **if you have no delight in her, then you shall let her go** where she will; but you shall not sell her at all for money. You shall not deal with her as a slave, because you have <u>**humbled her**</u>.

2**Cor 11:1** I wish that you would **bear with me in a little foolishness**, but indeed you do bear with me. **2** For I am <u>**jealous**</u> over you with a godly jealousy. For I espoused you to one **husband**, that I might present you as a pure virgin to Christ.

3 But I am afraid that somehow, as the <u>**serpent deceived Eve**</u> in his craftiness, so your minds might be corrupted from the simplicity that is in Christ. **4** For if he who comes preaches another Jesus whom we didn't preach, or **if you receive a different spirit which you didn't receive, or a different "good news" which you didn't accept**, you put up with that well enough. **5** For I reckon that I am not at all behind the very best apostles. **6** But though I am unskilled in speech, yet I am not unskilled in knowledge. No, in every way we have been revealed to you in all things.

7 Or did I commit a sin in <u>**humbling myself**</u> that you might be exalted, because I preached to you God's Good News free of charge?

NOTE: [Ki Tetze.] In Deuteronomy 21:14, a man at first believes the woman will be good for his household, but if, after a short time realizes she is not good for household and needs to "let her go." In the same way, Paul is afraid that the Corinthians have received teaching from "a different spirit" as if it were good news, when it is not, and even if they don't recognize it as good, they are letting it remain within their household, so to speak.

De 21:15 If a man has two wives, **the one beloved and the other hated**, and they have borne him children, both the beloved and the hated, and if the firstborn son is hers who was hated, **16** then it shall be, in the day that he causes his sons to inherit that which he has, that he may not give the son of the beloved the rights of the firstborn before the son of the hated, who is the firstborn; **17** but he shall acknowledge the firstborn, the son of the hated, <u>**by giving him a double portion of all that he has**</u>; for he is the beginning of his strength. The right of the firstborn is his.

2Cor 11:8 <u>I robbed other churches, taking wages from them that I might serve you</u>. **9** When I was present with you and was in need, I wasn't a burden to anyone, for the brothers, when they came from Macedonia, supplied the measure of my need. In everything I kept myself from being burdensome to you, and I will continue to do so. **10** As the truth of Christ is in me, no one will stop me from this boasting in the regions of Achaia. **11** Why? **Because I don't love you? God knows I do**!

NOTE: The echoes in this sectional pairing are swapped. Deuteronomy 21:15 echoing 2 Corinthians 11:11 may hint that Paul has found that the churches in Macedonia are a lot easier for Paul to love than the church in Corinth, nevertheless he loved Corinth too. But the pairing of Deut. 21:17 with 11:8 may also hint that Paul may feel he was compelled by God to bless Corinth bountifully. Paul's use of the word "robbed" is unusual – it is that Greek word's only appearance in the bible. Perhaps what Paul is implying is that while Macedonia was older in the faith than Corinth -- because Paul established a church there first (Acts 16:10), -- that he was nevertheless going out of his way to bless the younger "son" Corinth even more than the "firstborn" Macedonia!

De 21:18 If a man has a stubborn and rebellious son who will not obey the voice of his father or the voice of his mother, and though they chasten him, will not listen to them, **19** then his father and his mother shall take hold of him and bring him out to the elders of his city and to the gate of his place. **20** They shall tell the elders of his city, "This our son is stubborn and rebellious. He will not obey our voice. He is a glutton and a drunkard." **21** All the men of his city shall stone him to death with stones. **So you shall remove the evil from among you**. All Israel shall hear, and fear.

22 If a man has committed a sin worthy of death, and he is put to death, and you hang him on a tree, **23** his body shall not remain all night on the tree, but you shall surely bury him the same day; for he who is hanged is accursed of God. Don't defile your land which Yahweh your God gives you for an inheritance.

2Cor 11:12 But what I do, that I will continue to do, **that I may cut off opportunity from those who desire an opportunity**, that in which they boast, they may be recognized just like us. **13** For such men are false apostles, deceitful workers, masquerading as Christ's apostles. **14** And no wonder, for even Satan masquerades as an angel of light. **15** It is no great thing therefore if **his servants also masquerade as servants of righteousness, whose end will be according to their works**.

NOTE: By paying his own way, Paul's desire in 2 Cor.11:12 is to separate himself from the likeness of others who might hide wrong motives behind the desire to be paid by the saints. The echo in Deuteronomy is the command to remove the glutton and drunkard from among you, sins that are based in self-interest. Self-interest is the very thing from which Paul wants to disassociate himself.

Deuteronomy 22   2 Cor. 11:16

De 22:1 You shall not see your brother's ox or his sheep go astray and hide yourself from them. You shall surely bring them again to your brother. **2** If your brother isn't near to you, or if you don't know him, then you shall bring it home to your house, and it shall be with you until your brother comes seeking it, and you shall restore it to him. **3** So you shall do with his donkey, and so you shall do with his garment, and so you shall do with every lost thing of your brother's, which he has lost, and you have found. You may not hide yourself. **4** You shall not see your brother's donkey or his ox fallen down by the way, and hide yourself from them. You shall surely help him to lift them up again.

5 A woman shall not wear men's clothing, neither shall a man put on women's clothing; for whoever does these things is an abomination to Yahweh your God.

6 If you come across a bird's nest on the way, in any tree or on the ground, with young ones or eggs, and the hen is sitting on the young, or on the eggs, you shall not take the hen with the young. **7** You shall surely let the hen go, but the young you may take for yourself, that it may be well with you, and that you may prolong your days.

8 When you build a new house, then you shall make a railing around your roof, so that you don't bring blood on your house if anyone falls from there.

9 You shall not sow your vineyard with two kinds of seed, lest all the fruit be forfeited, the seed which you have sown, and the increase of the vineyard.

10 You shall not plow with an ox and a donkey together.

11 You shall not wear a mixed fabric, wool and linen together.

2**Cor 11:16** I say again, **let no one think me foolish**. But if so, yet receive me as foolish, that I also may boast a little.

NOTE: Some of the directives in this portion of Deuteronomy are perplexing, such as the command not to create a garment of wool and linen together. Jewish teaching says that this is a divine statute (a *chok*) God created to test Jewish willingness to obey a command for the simple reason that God commanded it. To outsiders the command might well seem foolish, even though we know it is not foolish because God chose to include it among His commandments. It is also possible that Pauls' "think me foolish" echoes Deuteronomy 22:5.

De 22:12 You shall make yourselves **fringes** on the four corners of your cloak with which you cover yourself.	2**Cor 11:16** I say again, let no one think me foolish. But if so, yet receive me as foolish, that I also may **boast a little**. **17** That which I speak, I don't speak according to the Lord, but as in foolishness, in this confidence of boasting. **18** Seeing that many boast after the flesh, I will also boast.

NOTE: It is without doubt that the fringes of the garments are meant for public display, and are both a reminder to the wearer and the viewer that the person wearing them has the intention to walk in righteousness. In this sectional pairing, Paul echoes that by saying that he will "boast a little." Paul does not ask forgiveness for this boasting, in the same way that he would not tell a Jew to conceal his tzitzit, so they are no longer visible, even though it is possible for them to be worn with prideful motives. Of course wrong motives are not only possible when obeying commands about one's physical appearance; it is possible for many kinds of commands to be obeyed with improper motives.

De 22:13 If any man takes a wife, and goes in to her, and hates her, **14** and accuses her of shameful things, and brings up an evil name on her, and says, "I took this woman, and when I came near to her, I didn't find in her the tokens of virginity," **15** then the young lady's father and mother shall take and bring the tokens of the young lady's virginity to the elders of the city in the gate. **16** The young lady's father shall say to the elders, "I gave my daughter to this man as wife, and he hates her. **17** Behold, he has accused her of shameful things, saying, 'I didn't find in your daughter the tokens of virginity;' and yet these are the tokens of my daughter's virginity." They shall spread the cloth before the elders of the city. **18** The elders of that city shall take the man and chastise him. **19** They shall fine him one hundred shekels of silver, and give them to the father of the young lady, because he has brought up an evil name on a virgin of Israel. She shall be his wife. He may not put her away all his days.

20 But if this thing is true, that the tokens of virginity were not found in the young lady, **21** then they shall bring out the young lady to the door of her father's house, and the men of her city shall stone her to death with stones, because she has done folly in Israel, to play the prostitute in her father's house. So you shall remove the evil from among you.

22 If a man is found lying with a woman married to a husband, then they shall both die, the man who lay with her and the woman. So you shall remove the evil from Israel.

23 If there is a young lady who is a virgin pledged to be married to a husband, and a man finds her in the city, and lies with her, **24** then you shall bring them both out to the gate of that city, and you shall stone them to death with stones; the lady, because she didn't cry, being in the city; and the man, because he has humbled his neighbor's wife. So you shall remove the evil from among you.

25 But if the man finds the lady who is pledged to be married in the field, and the man forces her and lies with her, then only the man who lay with her shall die. **26** But to the lady you shall do nothing. There is in the lady no sin worthy of death; for as when a man rises against his neighbor and kills him, even so is this matter; **27** for he found her in the field, the pledged to be married lady cried, and there was no one to save her.

2Cor **11:19** For you bear with the foolish gladly, being wise.

NOTE: Deuteronomy now lists a number of foolish actions and prescribes punishment for them. Apparently in Paul's view, the Corinthians are allowing foolish (sinful) things to occur and are taking *no action* to prevent it, while claiming to be making those decision in wisdom.

De 22:28 If a man finds a lady who is a virgin, who is not pledged to be married, and lays hold on her, and lies with her, and they are found, **29** then the man who lay with her shall give to the lady's father fifty shekels of silver. She shall be his wife, because he has humbled her. He may not put her away all his days. **30** A man shall not take his father's wife, and shall not uncover his father's skirt.	2**Cor 11:19** For you bear with the foolish gladly, being wise.

NOTE: This pairing is a continuation of the previous pairing.

Deuteronomy 23   2 Cor. 11:20

De 23:1 He who is emasculated by crushing or cutting shall not enter into Yahweh's assembly. **2** A person born of a **forbidden union** shall not enter into Yahweh's assembly; even to the tenth generation shall none of his enter into Yahweh's assembly. **3** An Ammonite or a Moabite shall not enter into Yahweh's assembly; even to the tenth generation shall none belonging to them enter into Yahweh's assembly forever, **4** because they **didn't meet you with bread and with water** on the way when *you came out of Egypt*, and because they hired against you **Balaam the son of Beor** from Pethor of Mesopotamia, to curse you. **5** Nevertheless Yahweh your God wouldn't listen to Balaam, but Yahweh your God **turned the curse into a blessing** to you, because Yahweh your God loved you. **6** You shall not seek their peace nor their prosperity all your days forever.	2**Cor 11:20** For you bear with a man if he **brings you into bondage**, if he **devours you**, if he *takes you captive*, if he **exalts himself**, or if he **strikes you on the face**.

NOTE: All of the main points in 2 Corinthians 11:20 seem to be found in these first verses of Deuteronomy Ch. 23. The full opposite of "giving of bread and water" is to devour them instead (echo 2). It was in Egypt that they were held captive (echo 3). Balaam exalted himself during the process of giving prophetic words, as discussed in the pairing notes of 1 Corinthians 13, and Numbers 22 (echo 4). The final echo five "strikes you on the face" being connected to Deut. 23:5 recalls two verses to mind: Matthew 5:39 concerning turning the other cheek when struck, and Romans 12:14 "Bless those who persecute you, bless and do not curse."

De 23:7 You shall not abhor an Edomite, for he is your brother. You shall not abhor an Egyptian, because you lived as a foreigner in his land. **8** The children of the third generation who are born to them may enter into Yahweh's assembly.

9 When you go out and camp against your enemies, then you shall keep yourselves from every evil thing.

10 If there is among you any man who is not clean by reason of that which happens to him by night, then shall he go outside of the camp. He shall not come within the camp; **11** but it shall be, when evening comes, he shall bathe himself in water. When the sun is down, he shall come within the camp.

12 You shall have a place also outside of the camp where you go relieve yourself. **13** You shall have a paddle among your weapons. It shall be, when you relieve yourself, you shall dig with it, and shall turn back and cover your excrement; **14** for Yahweh your God walks in the middle of your camp, to deliver you, and to give up your enemies before you. Therefore your camp shall be holy, that he may not see an unclean thing in you, and turn away from you.

NOTE: These verses seem to be skipped by Paul.

De 23:15 You shall not deliver to his master a servant who has escaped from his master to you. **16** He shall dwell with you, in the middle of you, in the place which he shall choose within one of your gates, where it pleases him best. **You shall not oppress him**.

17 There shall be no prostitute of the daughters of Israel, neither shall there be a sodomite of the sons of Israel. **18** You shall not bring the hire of a prostitute, or the wages of a male prostitute, into the house of Yahweh your God for any vow; for both of these are an abomination to Yahweh your God.

19 You shall not lend on interest to your brother: interest of money, interest of food, interest of anything that is lent on interest. **20** You may charge a foreigner interest; but you shall not charge your brother interest, that Yahweh your God may bless you in all that you put your hand to, in the land where you go in to possess it.

2Cor 11:20
For you bear with a man if he **brings you into bondage**, if he devours you, if he takes you captive, if he exalts himself, or if he strikes you on the face.

NOTE: Although all of the five main actions in 2 Corinthians 11:20 are echoed already in Deut. 23:1-6, those actions are found to be echoed again in the following passages in consecutive order, this time with clear instructions in Deuteronomy not to do these things to others. The first one, *bringing another into bondage* is present here. The others will follow in subsequent pairings.

De 23:21 When you vow a vow to Yahweh your God, you shall not be slack to pay it; for Yahweh your God will surely require it of you, and it would be sin in you. **22** But if you refrain from vowing, it shall be no sin in you. **23** That which has gone out of your lips you shall observe and do. According as you have vowed to Yahweh your God, a free will offering, which you have promised with your mouth.

24 When you come into your neighbor's vineyard, then you may eat your fill of grapes at your own pleasure; but you shall not put any in your container.

25 When you come into your neighbor's standing grain, then you may pluck the ears with your hand; but you shall not use a sickle on your neighbor's standing grain.

2**Cor 11:20** For you bear with a man if he brings you into bondage, if he **devours you**, if he takes you captive, if he exalts himself, or if he strikes you on the face.

NOTE: The second action of 2 Corinthians 11:20, *devours you,* is echoed in Deuteronomy 23:24.

Deuteronomy 24

De 24:1 When a man takes a wife and marries her, then it shall be, if she finds no favor in his eyes because he has found some unseemly thing in her, that he shall write her a bill of divorce, give it in her hand, and send her out of his house. **2** When she has departed out of his house, she may go and be another man's wife. **3** If the latter husband hates her, and writes her a bill of divorce, gives it in her hand, and sends her out of his house; or if the latter husband dies, who took her to be his wife, **4** her former husband, who sent her away, may not take her again to be his wife after she is defiled; for that would be an abomination to Yahweh. You shall not cause the land to sin, which Yahweh your God gives you for an inheritance.

5 When a man takes a new wife, he shall not go out in the army, neither shall he be assigned any business. He shall be free at home one year and shall cheer his wife whom he has taken.

NOTE: Having already discussed marriage issues in his first letter to the Corinthians (1 Cor. Ch.7), these verses seem to be skipped by Paul.

De 24:6 No man shall take the mill or the upper millstone as a pledge, for he takes a life in pledge.

7 If a man is found stealing any of his brothers of the children of Israel, **and he deals with him as a slave, or sells him, then that thief shall die**. So you shall remove the evil from among you.

8 Be careful in the plague of leprosy, that you observe diligently and do according to all that the Levitical priests teach you. As I commanded them, so you shall observe to do. **9** Remember what Yahweh your God did to Miriam, by the way as you came out of Egypt.

10 When you lend your neighbor any kind of loan, **you shall not go into his house to get his pledge**. **11** You shall stand outside, and the man to whom you lend shall bring the pledge outside to you. **12** If he is a poor man, you shall not sleep with his pledge. **13** You shall surely restore to him the pledge when the sun goes down, that he may sleep in his garment and bless you. It shall be righteousness to you before Yahweh your God.

14 You shall not oppress a hired servant who is poor and needy, whether he is one of your brothers or one of the foreigners who are in your land within your gates. **15** In his day you shall give him his hire, neither shall the sun go down on it, for he is poor and sets his heart on it, lest he cry against you to Yahweh, and it be sin to you.

16 The fathers shall not be put to death for the children, neither shall the children be put to death for the fathers. Every man shall be put to death for his own sin.

17 You shall not deprive the foreigner or the fatherless of justice, nor take a widow's clothing in pledge; **18** but you shall remember that you were a slave in Egypt, and Yahweh your God redeemed you there. Therefore I command you to do this thing.

19 When you reap your harvest in your field, and have forgotten a sheaf in the field, you shall not go again to get it. It shall be for the foreigner, for the fatherless, and for the widow, that Yahweh your God may bless you in all the work of your hands. **20** When you beat your olive tree, you shall not go over the boughs again. It shall be for the foreigner, for the fatherless, and for the widow.

21 When you harvest your vineyard, you shall not glean it after yourselves. It shall be for the foreigner, for the fatherless, and for the widow. **22** You shall remember that you were a slave in the land of Egypt. Therefore I command you to do this thing.

2**Cor 11:20** For you bear with a man if he brings you into bondage, if he devours you, if he **takes you captive**, if he **exalts himself**, or if he strikes you on the face.

NOTE: The third and fourth actions of 2 Corinthians 11:20, *take captive* and *exalting* are echoed here.

Deuteronomy 25   2 Cor. 11:20

De 25:1 If there is a controversy between men, and they come to judgment and the judges judge them, then they shall justify the righteous and condemn the wicked. **2** It shall be, if the wicked man is worthy to be beaten, that the judge shall cause him to lie down and to be beaten before his face, according to his wickedness, by number. **3** He may sentence him to no more than forty stripes. He shall not exceed, lest if he should exceed, and beat him above these with many stripes, then your brother would be degraded in your sight.

4 You shall not muzzle the ox when he treads out the grain.

5 If brothers dwell together, and one of them dies and has no son, the wife of the dead shall not be married outside to a stranger. Her husband's brother shall go in to her, and take her as his wife, and perform the duty of a husband's brother to her. **6** It shall be that the firstborn whom she bears shall succeed in the name of his brother who is dead, that his name not be blotted out of Israel. **7** If the man doesn't want to take his brother's wife, then his brother's wife shall go up to the gate to the elders, and say, "My husband's brother refuses to raise up to his brother a name in Israel. He will not perform the duty of a husband's brother to me." **8** Then the elders of his city shall call him, and speak to him. If he stands and says, "I don't want to take her," **9** then his brother's wife shall come to him in the presence of the elders, and loose his shoe from off his foot, and spit in his face. She shall answer and say, "So shall it be done to the man who does not build up his brother's house." **10** His name shall be called in Israel, "The house of him who had his shoe loosened."

11 When men strive together, one with another, and the wife of the one draws near to **deliver her husband out of the hand of him who strikes him**, and puts out her hand, and takes him by his private parts, **12** then you shall cut off her hand. Your eye shall have no pity.

2**Cor 11:20** For you bear with a man if he brings you into bondage, if he devours you, if he takes you captive, if he exalts himself, or if he **strikes you** on the face.

NOTE: The fifth and final action of 2 Corinthians 11:20, *strike the face* is echoed here. The words *hand* and *strike*, are present, and the word *eye* in Deuteronomy 25;12 might have inspired Paul to write the word *face*.

De 25:13 You shall not have in your bag diverse weights, one heavy and one light. **14** You shall not have in your house diverse measures, one large and one small. **15** You shall have a perfect and just weight. You shall have a perfect and just measure, that your days may be long in the land which Yahweh your God gives you. **16** For all who do such things, all who do unrighteously, are an abomination to Yahweh your God.

17 Remember what Amalek did to you by the way as you came out of Egypt, **18** how he met you by the way, and struck the rearmost of you, all who were feeble behind you, **when you were faint and weary**; and he didn't fear God. **19** Therefore it shall be, when Yahweh your God has given you rest from all your enemies all around, in the land which Yahweh your God gives you for an inheritance to possess it, **that you shall blot out the memory of Amalek from under the sky**. You shall not forget.

2Cor 11:21a I speak by way of disparagement, **as though we had been weak**.

11:21b Yet in whatever way anyone is bold (I say it in foolishness), I am bold also.

NOTE: [Ki Tetze ends.] In 2 Corinthians 11:21a, Paul echoes the idea that the Corinthians are being abused by those around them, even as the Amalekites abused the Children of Israel. And Paul's phrase "as though we had been weak" might have been inspired by the circumstances of Moses, who became tired while raising his hands and needed help to do so. Was Moses, therefore, weak? No! But he might have been accused of weakness because of the circumstances. Is Paul perhaps cognizant of the fact that the Corinthians weaknesses were being seen by some as a reflection of his weakness as an Apostle? In 2 Cor. 11:21b, Paul may be saying this based on this principle: to the extent that Amalek is bold enough to say it will ultimately destroy Israel, Moses commands Israel to be bold enough to say that the memory of Amalek shall be blotted out.

Deuteronomy 26 | 2 Cor. 11:22

De 26:1 It shall be, when you have come in to the land which Yahweh your God gives you for an inheritance, possess it, and dwell in it, **2** that you shall take some of the first of all the fruit of the ground, which you shall bring in from your land that Yahweh your God gives you. You shall put it in a basket, and shall go to the place which Yahweh your God shall choose to cause his name to dwell there. **3** You shall come to the priest who shall be in those days, and tell him, "I profess today to Yahweh your God, that I have come to the land which Yahweh swore to our fathers to give us." **4** The priest shall take the basket out of your hand, and set it down before the altar of Yahweh your God. **5** You shall answer and say before Yahweh your God, "**A Syrian ready to perish was my father**. He went down into Egypt, and lived there, few in number. There **he became a great, mighty, and populous nation**. 6 The Egyptians mistreated us, afflicted us, and imposed hard labor on us. 7 Then we cried to Yahweh, the God **of our fathers**. Yahweh heard our voice, and saw our affliction, our toil, and our oppression. 8 Yahweh brought us out of Egypt with a mighty hand, with an outstretched arm, with great terror, with signs, and with wonders; **9** and he has brought us into this place, and has given us this land, a land flowing with milk and honey. **10** Now, behold, I have brought the first of the fruit of the ground, which you, Yahweh, have given me." You shall set it down before Yahweh your God, and worship before Yahweh your God. **11** You shall rejoice in all the good which Yahweh your God has given to you, and to your house, you, and the Levite, and the foreigner who is among you.

2Cor 11:22 **Are they Hebrews**?
So am I.

Are they Israelites?
So am I.

Are they the **offspring of Abraham**? So am I.

NOTE: [Ki Tavo.] Regarding Deuteronomy 26:5, Other translations say, "My father was a wandering Aramean." This has long been attributed to Abraham, who was a Hebrew, descendent of Eber, meaning "to cross over." But it was Jacob, more properly Israel, that became a populous nation.

De 26:12 When you have finished tithing all the tithe of your increase in the third year, which is the year of tithing, then you shall give it to the Levite, to the foreigner, to the fatherless, and to the widow, that they may eat within your gates and be filled. **13** You shall say before Yahweh your God, "I have put away the holy things out of my house, and also have given them to the Levite, to the foreigner, to the fatherless, and to the widow, according to all your commandment which you have commanded me. I have not transgressed any of your commandments, neither have I forgotten them. **14** I have not eaten of it in my mourning, neither have I removed any of it while I was unclean, nor given of it for the dead. I have listened to Yahweh my God's voice. I have done according to all that you have commanded me. **15** Look down from your holy habitation, from heaven, and bless your people Israel, and the ground which you have given us, as you swore to our fathers, a land flowing with milk and honey."

16 This day Yahweh your God commands you to do these statutes and ordinances. You shall keep and do them with all your heart and with all your soul. **17 You have declared today that Yahweh is your God, and that you would walk in his ways, keep his statutes, his commandments, and his ordinances, and listen to his voice**. **18** Yahweh has declared today that you are a people for his own possession, as he has promised you, and that you should keep all his commandments. **19 He will make you high above all nations that he has made, in praise, in name, and in honor, and that you may be a holy people to Yahweh your God, as he has spoken**.

2Cor 11:23 **Are they servants of Christ**? (I speak as one beside himself) I am more so: in labors more abundantly, in prisons more abundantly, in stripes above measure, in deaths often.

NOTE: Deuteronomy 26:19 is almost unique in the Torah in the way God promises their glory. Paul tempers his own echo by calling himself "out of his own mind" as he is about to brag about how miserably he has been treated, in comparison to the loftiness of Deut. 26:19!

Deuteronomy 27

2 Cor. 11:23

De 27:1 Moses and the elders of Israel commanded the people, saying, "Keep all the commandment which I command you today. **2** It shall be on the day when you shall pass over the Jordan to the land which Yahweh your God gives you, that you shall set yourself up great **stones**, and coat them with plaster. **3** You shall write on them all the words of this law, when you have passed over, that you may go in to the land which Yahweh your God gives you, a land flowing with milk and honey, as Yahweh, the God of your fathers, has promised you. **4** It shall be, when you have crossed over the Jordan, that you shall set up these **stones**, which I command you today, in Mount Ebal, and you shall coat them with plaster. **5** There you shall build an altar to Yahweh your God, an altar of **stones**. You shall not use any iron tool on them. **6** You shall build Yahweh your God's altar of **uncut stones**. You shall offer burnt offerings on it to Yahweh your God. **7** You shall sacrifice peace offerings, and shall eat there. You shall rejoice before Yahweh your God. **8** You shall write on the stones all the words of this law very plainly."

9 Moses and the Levitical priests spoke to all Israel, saying, "Be silent and listen, Israel! Today you have become the people of Yahweh your God. **10** You shall therefore obey the voice of Yahweh your God, and do his commandments and his statutes, which I command you today."

2**Cor 11:23** Are they servants of Christ? (I speak as one beside himself) I am more so:

in **labors more** abundantly, in **prisons more** abundantly, in **stripes above** measure, in **deaths often**.

NOTE: This pairing begins another sequence of sectional pairings in which Paul again lists the counts of items in Deuteronomy that match the same counts in his lists in 2 Corinthians. (See the notes under Deut. 12:1 for earlier examples).

NOTE: The fifth use of the word "stones" in Deuteronomy 27:8, will be discussed in the notes below 2 Corinthians 11:25.

De 27:11 Moses commanded the people the same day, saying, **12** "These shall stand on Mount Gerizim to bless the people, when you have crossed over the Jordan: Simeon, Levi, Judah, Issachar, Joseph, and Benjamin. **13** These shall stand on Mount Ebal for the curse: Reuben, Gad, Asher, Zebulun, Dan, and Naphtali. **14** The Levites shall answer, and say to all the men of Israel with a loud voice,

15 'Cursed is the man who makes an engraved or molten image, an abomination to Yahweh, the work of the hands of the craftsman, and sets it up in secret.' All the people shall answer and say, 'Amen.'

16 'Cursed is he who dishonors his father or his mother.' All the people shall say, 'Amen.'

17 'Cursed is he who removes his neighbor's landmark.' All the people shall say, 'Amen.'

18 'Cursed is he who leads the blind astray on the road.' All the people shall say, 'Amen.'

19 'Cursed is he who withholds justice from the foreigner, fatherless, and widow.' All the people shall say, 'Amen.'

20 'Cursed is he who lies with his father's wife, because he dishonors his father's bed.' All the people shall say, 'Amen.'

21 'Cursed is he who lies with any kind of animal.' All the people shall say, 'Amen.'

22 'Cursed is he who lies with his sister, the daughter of his father, or the daughter of his mother.' All the people shall say, 'Amen.'

23 'Cursed is he who lies with his mother-in-law.' All the people shall say, 'Amen.'

24 'Cursed is he who strikes his neighbor in secret.' All the people shall say, 'Amen.'

25 'Cursed is he who takes a bribe to kill an innocent person.' All the people shall say, 'Amen.'

26 'Cursed is he who doesn't uphold the words of this law by doing them.' All the people shall say, 'Amen.'"

2Cor 11:24 Five times I received forty stripes minus one from the Jews. **25a** Three times I was beaten with rods. Once I was stoned. Three times I suffered shipwreck.

NOTE: The word "cursed" is used here twelve times. Paul's list is of twelve persecutions: 5 + 3 + 1 + 3 = 12.

| De 27:8 You shall write on the stones all the words of this law very plainly." | 2Cor 11:25b I have been a night and a day in the deep. |

NOTE: The echo of Deuteronomy 27:8 is found to be out of order in 2 Corinthians in this highly unusual echo! We should have expected this echo to be stated at the end of 2 Corinthians 11:23, not at the end of 2 Cor. 11:25. This placement at the end of verse 11:25 breaks the parallelism of the numbering! Why did Paul add this stand-alone thought here, and not earlier? One possible explanation is his humility. Even though Deut. 27:1-8 had five mentions of the word "stones" not just four, Paul could not bring himself to exalt himself with the fifth mention of stones – a mention that included the writing of the Torah itself, something that God wrote with his finger. But after finding in his life a complete parallelism with all twelve curses, he had peace from God to add the echo, albeit out of order.

Deuteronomy 28   2 Cor. 11:26

De 28:1 It shall happen, if you shall listen diligently to Yahweh your God's voice, to observe to do all his commandments which I command you today, that Yahweh your God will set you high above all the nations of the earth. **2** All these blessings will come upon you, and overtake you, if you listen to Yahweh your God's voice.

3 You shall be blessed in the city, and you shall be blessed in the field.

4 You shall be blessed in the fruit of your body, the fruit of your ground, the fruit of your animals, the increase of your livestock, and the young of your flock.

5 Your basket and your kneading trough shall be blessed.

6 You shall be blessed when you come in, and you shall be blessed when you go out.

7 Yahweh will cause your enemies who rise up against you to be struck before you. They will come out against you one way, and will flee before you seven ways. **8** Yahweh will command the blessing on you in your barns, and in all that you put your hand to. He will bless you in the land which Yahweh your God gives you. **9** Yahweh will establish you for a holy people to himself, as he has sworn to you, if you shall keep the commandments of Yahweh your God, and walk in his ways. **10** All the peoples of the earth shall see that you are called by Yahweh's name, and they will be afraid of you. **11** Yahweh will grant you abundant prosperity in the fruit of your body, in the fruit of your livestock, and in the fruit of your ground, in the land which Yahweh swore to your fathers to give you. **12** Yahweh will open to you his good treasure in the sky, to give the rain of your land in its season, and to bless all the work of your hand. You will lend to many nations, and you will not borrow. **13** Yahweh will make you the head, and not the tail. You will be above only, and you will not be beneath, if you listen to the commandments of Yahweh your God which I command you today, to observe and to do, **14** and shall not turn away from any of the words which I command you today, to the right hand or to the left, to go after other gods to serve them.

2**Cor** 11:26 I have been in travels often, perils of rivers, perils of robbers, perils from my countrymen, perils from the Gentiles,

perils in the city, perils in the wilderness,

perils in the sea, perils among false brothers;

NOTE: Eight uses of the word *bless* echo the eight kinds of *perils* Paul as faced. This is reminiscent of Paul's treatment of the Priestly blessing in Numbers 6:22 in which Paul chooses not to retell of his blessings, but rather how they bless others even when persecuted. But this time Paul echoes "blessing" with the opposite idea: "perils," the occurrences of natural or human forces that threaten to slow or stop the expansion of the gospel.

De 28:15 But it shall come to pass, if you will not listen to Yahweh your God's voice, to observe to do all his commandments and his statutes which I command you today, that all these curses will come on you and overtake you.

16 You will be **cursed** in the city, and you will be <u>cursed</u> in the field.

17 Your basket and your kneading trough will be **cursed**.

18 The fruit of your body, the fruit of your ground, the increase of your livestock, and the young of your flock will be **<u>cursed</u>**.

19 You will be <u>cursed</u> when you come in, and you will be **<u>cursed</u>** when you go out.

2Cor 11:27 in **weariness and painfulness**, in <u>watchings often</u>, in **hunger and thirst**, in **<u>fastings often</u>**, and in <u>cold and nakedness</u>. **28** Besides those things that are outside, there is that which presses on me daily: **<u>anxiety for all the churches</u>**.

NOTE: Six uses of the word "cursed" seem to echo Paul's six kinds of physical pressures. Those are: weariness and painfulness, watchings often (sleepless nights), hunger and thirst, fastings often, cold and nakedness, anxiety for all the churches. Each of these six pressures are either two words long, or include plural concepts. This echoes the group nature of the curses in Deuteronomy.

De 28:20 Yahweh will send on you cursing, confusion, and rebuke in all that you put your hand to do, until you are destroyed and until you perish quickly, because of the evil of your doings, by which you have forsaken me. **21** Yahweh will make the pestilence cling to you, until he has consumed you from off the land where you go in to possess it. **22** Yahweh will strike you with consumption, with fever, with inflammation, with fiery heat, with the sword, with blight, and with mildew. They will pursue you until you perish. **23** Your sky that is over your head will be bronze, and the earth that is under you will be iron. **24** Yahweh will make the rain of your land powder and dust. It will come down on you from the sky, until you are destroyed.

25 Yahweh will cause you to be struck before your enemies. You will go out one way against them, and will flee seven ways before them. You will be tossed back and forth among all the kingdoms of the earth. **26** Your dead bodies will be food to all birds of the sky, and to the animals of the earth; and there will be no one to frighten them away.

27 Yahweh will strike you with the boils of Egypt, with tumors, with the scurvy, and with the itch, of which you cannot be healed. **28** Yahweh will strike you with madness, with blindness, and with astonishment of heart. **29** You will grope at noonday, as the blind gropes in darkness, and you shall not prosper in your ways. You will only be oppressed and robbed always, and there will be no one to save you. **30** You will betroth a wife, and another man shall lie with her. You will build a house, and you won't dwell in it. You will plant a vineyard, and not use its fruit. **31** Your ox will be slain before your eyes, and you will not eat of it. Your donkey will be violently taken away from before your face, and will not be restored to you. Your sheep will be given to your enemies, and you will have no one to save you. **32** Your sons and your daughters will be given to another people. Your eyes will look, and fail with longing for them all day long. There will be no power in your hand. **33** A nation which you don't know will eat the fruit of your ground and all your work. You will only be oppressed and crushed always, **34** so that the sights that you see with your eyes will drive you mad. **35** Yahweh will strike you in the knees and in the legs with a sore boil, of which you cannot be healed, from the sole of your foot to the crown of your head. **36** Yahweh will bring you, and your king whom you shall set over you, to a nation that you have not known, you nor your fathers. There you will serve other gods, wood and stone. **37** You will become an astonishment, a proverb, and a byword among all the peoples where Yahweh will lead you away.

NOTE: These verses seem to be skipped by Paul.

De 28:38 You will carry much seed out into the field, and will gather little in, for the locust will consume it. **39** You will plant vineyards and dress them, but you will neither drink of the wine, nor harvest, because worms will eat them. **40** You will have olive trees throughout all your borders, but you won't anoint yourself with the oil, for your olives will drop off. **41** You will father sons and daughters, but they will not be yours, for they will go into captivity. **42** All your trees and the fruit of your ground will be devoured by the locust. **43** The foreigner who is among you will mount up above you higher and higher, and you will come down lower and lower. **44** He will lend to you, and you won't lend to him. He will be the head, and you will be the tail.

45 All these curses will come on you, and will pursue you and overtake you, until you are destroyed, because you didn't listen to Yahweh your God's voice, to keep his commandments and his statutes which he commanded you. **46** They will be for a sign and for a wonder to you and to your offspring forever.

NOTE: These verses seem to be skipped by Paul.

De 28:47 Because you didn't serve Yahweh your God with joyfulness and with gladness of heart, by reason of the abundance of all things; **48** therefore you will serve your enemies whom Yahweh sends against you, **in hunger, in thirst, in nakedness, and in lack of all things**. He will put an iron yoke on your neck until he has destroyed you.

49 Yahweh will bring a nation against you from far away, from the end of the earth, as the eagle flies; **a nation whose language you will not understand**,

2Cor 11:29 Who **is weak, and I am not weak**?

Who is **caused to stumble, and I don't burn with indignation**?

NOTE: Stumbling of various kinds is inevitable when communication is lacking.

De 28:50 a nation of **fierce facial expressions**, that doesn't respect the elderly, nor show favor to the young. **51** They will eat the fruit of your livestock and the fruit of your ground, until you are destroyed. They also won't leave you grain, new wine, oil, the increase of your livestock, or the young of your flock, until they have caused you to perish. **52** They will **besiege you in all your gates** until your **high and fortified walls in which you trusted come down** throughout all your land. They will besiege you in all your gates throughout all your land which Yahweh your God has given you.

2Cor 11:30 If I must boast, I will boast of the things that concern my weakness. **31** The God and Father of the Lord Jesus Christ, he who is blessed forevermore, knows that I don't lie. **32** In Damascus **the governor under King Aretas guarded the city of the Damascenes** desiring to arrest me. **33 I was let down in a basket through a window by the wall**, and escaped his hands.

NOTE: Paul's direct, personal mention of one of his adversaries in 2 Corinthians 11:32 may echo the very direction and personal mention of "facial expressions" of the oppressors of Israel in Deuteronomy 28:50.

De 28:53 You will eat the fruit of your own body, the flesh of your sons and of your daughters, whom Yahweh your God has given you, in the siege and in the distress with which your enemies will distress you. **54** The man who is tender among you, and very delicate, his eye will be evil toward his brother, toward the wife whom he loves, and toward the remnant of his children whom he has remaining, **55** so that he will not give to any of them of the flesh of his children whom he will eat, because he has nothing left to him, in the siege and in the distress with which your enemy will distress you in all your gates. **56** The tender and delicate woman among you, who would not venture to set the sole of her foot on the ground for delicateness and tenderness, her eye will be evil toward the husband that she loves, toward her son, toward her daughter, **57** toward her young one who comes out from between her feet, and toward her children whom she shall bear; for she will eat them secretly for lack of all things in the siege and in the distress with which your enemy will distress you in your gates.

58 If you will not observe to do all the words of this law that are written in this book, that you may fear this glorious and fearful name, YAHWEH YOUR GOD, **59** then Yahweh will make your plagues and the plagues of your offspring fearful, even great plagues, and of long duration, and severe sicknesses, and of long duration. **60** He will bring on you again all the diseases of Egypt, which you were afraid of; and they will cling to you. **61** Also every sickness and every plague which is not written in the book of this law, Yahweh will bring them on you until you are destroyed. **62** You will be left few in number, whereas you were as the stars of the sky for multitude, because you didn't listen to Yahweh your God's voice. **63** It will happen that as Yahweh rejoiced over you to do you good, and to multiply you, so Yahweh will rejoice over you to cause you to perish and to destroy you. You will be plucked from the land where you go in to possess it. **64** Yahweh will scatter you among all peoples, from one end of the earth to the other end of the earth. There you will serve other gods which you have not known, you nor your fathers, even wood and stone. **65** Among these nations you will find no ease, and there will be no rest for the sole of your foot; but Yahweh will give you there a trembling heart, failing of eyes, and pining of soul. **66** Your life will hang in doubt before you. You will be afraid night and day, and will have no assurance of your life. **67** In the morning you will say, "I wish it were evening!" and at evening you will say, "I wish it were morning!" for the fear of your heart which you will fear, and for the sight of your eyes which you will see. **68** Yahweh will bring you into Egypt again with ships, by the way of which I said to you, "You will never see it again." There you will offer yourselves for sale to your enemies as male and female slaves, but no one will buy you.

NOTE: These verses seem to be skipped by Paul.

Deuteronomy 29

2 Corinthians 12

De 29:1 These are the words of the covenant which Yahweh commanded Moses to make with the children of Israel in the land of Moab, in addition to the covenant which he made with them in Horeb.

2 Moses called to all Israel, and said to them, "**You have seen all that Yahweh did before your eyes in the land of Egypt** to Pharaoh, and to all his servants, and to all his land; **3** the great trials which your eyes saw, the signs, and those <u>great wonders</u>. **4** But **Yahweh has not given you a heart to know**, _eyes to see_, and **ears to hear**, to this day. **5** I have led you forty years in the wilderness. Your clothes have not grown old on you, and your sandals have not grown old on your feet. **6** You have not eaten bread, neither have you drunk wine or strong drink, that you may know that I am Yahweh your God. **7** When you came to this place, Sihon the king of Heshbon and Og the king of Bashan came out against us to battle, and we struck them. **8** We took their land, and gave it for an inheritance to the Reubenites, and to the Gadites, and to the half-tribe of the Manassites. **9** <u>**Therefore keep the words of this covenant and do them, that you may prosper in all that you do**</u>.

2Cor 12:1 It is doubtless not profitable for me to boast, **but I will come to visions and revelations** of the Lord.

2 I know a man in Christ who was <u>caught up into the third heaven fourteen years ago</u>—whether in the body, I don't know, or whether out of the body, I don't know; God knows. **3** I know such a man (whether in the body, or outside of the body, **I don't know; God knows**), **4** how he was _caught up into Paradise_ and **heard unspeakable words**, which it is not lawful for a man to utter. **5** On behalf of such a one I will boast, but on my own behalf I will not boast, except in my weaknesses. **6** <u>For if I would desire to boast, I will not be foolish; for I will speak the truth. But I refrain</u>, so that no man may think more of me than that which he sees in me or hears from me.

NOTE: [Ki Tavo ends.] In 2 Corinthians 12:2, the word "man" might echo Pharoah, who himself saw great wonders of God. In Deuteronomy 29:9, although the victory over Sihon and Og was tremendous, Moses does not boast about it nor record the details of the victory in words, but simply uses the victory as motivation to keep the covenant.

De 29:10 You <u>**stand today, all of you, before Yahweh your God: your heads, your tribes, your elders, and your officers, even all the men of Israel**</u>, **11** your little ones, your wives, and the foreigners who are in the middle of your camps, from the one who cuts your wood to the one who draws your water, **12** that you may **enter into the covenant of Yahweh your God, and into his oath**, which Yahweh your God makes with you today, **13** that he may establish you today as a people to himself, and that he may be your God, as he spoke to you and as he swore to your fathers, to Abraham, to Isaac, and to Jacob.

14 Neither do I make this covenant and this oath with you only, **15** but with those who <u>**stand**</u> here with us today before Yahweh our God, and also with those who are not here with us today

2Cor 12:7a By reason of the exceeding **greatness** of the **revelations**, I should not be **exalted** **excessively**,

NOTE: [Nitzavim.] The word "stand" in Deuteronomy 29:15 is most commonly translated "appointed" or "arise," which Paul echoes with "exalted excessively." Paul sees context to speak personally about himself at his moment, because that same verse includes descendants, "and also with those who are not here with us today." The Deuteronomy side of this pairing references "standing" three times with unique Hebrew words: 29:10 "stand," (Heb: natsab) 29:13 "establish," (Heb: qum), and 29:15 "stand" (Heb: amad).

De 29:16 (for you know how we lived in the land of Egypt, and how we came through the middle of the nations through which you passed; **17** and you have seen their abominations and their idols, wood and stone, silver and gold, which were among them); **18** lest there should be among you man, woman, family, or tribe whose heart turns away today from Yahweh our God, to go to serve the gods of those nations; lest there should be among you a **root that produces bitter poison**; **19** and it happen, when he hears the words of this curse, that he bless himself in his heart, saying, "I shall have peace, though I walk in the stubbornness of my heart," to destroy the moist with the dry. **20** Yahweh will not pardon him, but then **Yahweh's anger and his jealousy will smoke against that man**, and all the curse that is written in this book will lie on him, and Yahweh will blot out his name from under the sky. **21** Yahweh will set him apart for evil out of all the tribes of Israel, according to all the curses of the covenant written in this book of the law.

2Cor 12:7b

a **thorn in the flesh** was given to me:

a **messenger of Satan to torment me,**

that I should **not be exalted excessively**.

NOTE: The well-known "thorn in the flesh" statement of Paul finds its echo here in the idea in Deuteronomy 29:18 that evil in the nation can become a poisonous root that destroys many. God knows what Paul does not – that Paul will be used to influence billions of people in the millennia to come. Any misstep could poison the people of God. Thus in Deut. 29:20 God's promises to get personally involved against "that man" with a "smoke" or burning that does not cease. And in Deut. 29:21 the word "evil" is commonly translated "adversity."

De 29:16 (for you know how we lived in the land of Egypt, and how we came through the middle of the nations through which you passed; **17** and you have seen their abominations and their idols, wood and stone, silver and gold, which were among them); **18** lest there should be among you man, woman, family, or tribe whose heart turns away today from Yahweh our God, to go to serve the gods of those nations; lest there should be among you a root that produces bitter poison; **19** and it happen, when he hears the words of this curse, that he bless himself in his heart, saying, "**I shall have peace**, though I walk in the stubbornness of my heart," to destroy the moist with the dry. **20** **Yahweh will not pardon him**, but then Yahweh's anger and his jealousy will smoke against that man, and all the curse that is written in this book will lie on him, and Yahweh will blot out his name from under the sky. **21** Yahweh will set him apart for evil out of all the tribes of Israel, according to all the curses of the covenant written in this book of the law.

2Cor 12:8 Concerning this thing, I **begged the Lord three times that it might depart from me.**

9 He has said to me, "**My grace is sufficient for you**, for my power is made perfect in weakness." Most gladly therefore I will rather glory in my weaknesses, that the power of Christ may rest on me.

NOTE: No wonder Paul was confused! He had never considered that God might take Deuteronomy 29:16-21 as *permission* to come against Paul directly, a man who had been fully faithful to the call he had been given! Paul wanted "peace" but did not get it. Why three times? See the notes under Deut. 29:10-15 for one possibility.

29:22 The generation to come—your children who will rise up after you, and the foreigner who will come from a far land—will say, when they see the **plagues of that land, and the sicknesses** with which Yahweh has made it sick, **23** that <u>all its land is sulfur, salt, and burning, that it is not sown, doesn't produce, nor does any grass grow in it</u>, like the overthrow of Sodom, Gomorrah, Admah, and Zeboiim, which Yahweh overthrew in his anger, and in his wrath. **24** Even all the nations will say, "Why has Yahweh done this to this land? What does the heat of this great anger mean?" **25** Then men will say, "Because they abandoned the covenant of Yahweh, the God of their fathers, which he made with them when he brought them out of the land of Egypt, **26** and went and served other gods and worshiped them, gods that they didn't know, and that he had not given to them. **27** Therefore Yahweh's **anger burned against this land, to bring on it all the curse that is written in this book. 28** Yahweh <u>rooted them out of their land</u> in anger, in wrath, and in great indignation, and **thrust them into another land**, as it is today.

29 <u>The secret things belong to Yahweh our God; but the things that are revealed belong to us</u> and to our children forever, that we may do all the words of this law.

2Cor 12:9 He has said to me, "My grace is sufficient for you, for my power is made perfect in weakness." Most gladly therefore I will rather glory in my weaknesses, that the power of Christ may rest on me. **10** Therefore I take pleasure in **weaknesses**, in <u>injuries</u>, in **necessities**, in <u>persecutions</u>, and in **distresses**, for Christ's sake. <u>For when I am weak, then am I strong</u>.

NOTE: In 2 Corinthians 12:10, "weaknesses" can also be translated as *sickness*, *diseases* and *illness* (echo 1). Next, "injuries" can also be translated *insults*, or an act of *wanton violence* (echo 2). Next, "necessities" speaks towards an *inevitable result* echoed in "the curse written in this book" (echo 3). Next, "persecutions" [Gr: diogmos] is the same word used in Acts 8:1 that quickly caused the scattering (or uprooting) of the church (echo 4). Finally "distresses" literally means *narrowness of space* echoing "thrust them into another land" (echo 5). Paul's conclusion: "For when I am weak, then am I strong" is brilliantly echoed in Deuteronomy 29:29. Paul's word perfectly echoes "the things that are revealed belong to us." In other words it is the dramatic conclusion of his struggle to understand what God had hidden from him, which is *why* he was being tormented with a thorn in the flesh when he had done nothing wrong!

NOTE: Paul's phrase "glory in my weaknesses" in 2 Cor. 12:9 may have its echo in the Deut. 29:24 question of nations who ask why Yahweh has turned the land to ruin and in the Deut. 29:15 answer, "Because they abandoned the covenant of Yahweh, the God of their fathers." In other words, even in the weaknesses of God's people, God can still be glorified, and Paul can glory in his own weaknesses because he knows they can also be used to glorify God.

Deuteronomy 30   2 Cor. 12:11

De 30:1 It shall happen, when all these things have come on you, the blessing and the curse, which I have set before you, and you shall call them to mind **among all the nations where Yahweh your God has driven you**, 2 and return to Yahweh your God and obey his voice according to all that I command you today, you and your children, with all your heart and with all your soul, **3 that then Yahweh your God will release you from captivity, have compassion on you**, and will return and gather you from all the peoples where Yahweh your God has scattered you. **4** If your outcasts are in the uttermost parts of the heavens, from there Yahweh your God will gather you, and from there he will take you. **5** Yahweh your God will bring you into the land which your fathers possessed, and you will possess it. He will do you good, and increase your numbers **more than your fathers**.

6 Yahweh your **God will circumcise your heart**, and the heart of your offspring, to love Yahweh your God with all your heart and with all your soul, that you may live. **7 Yahweh your God will** put all these curses on **your enemies** and on **those who hate you**, who **persecuted you**. **8** You shall return and obey the voice of Yahweh, and do all his commandments which I command you today. **9** Yahweh your God will make you prosperous in all the work of your hand, in the fruit of your body, in the fruit of your livestock, and in the fruit of your ground, for good; for Yahweh will again rejoice over you for good, as he rejoiced over your fathers, **10** if you will obey the voice of Yahweh your God, to keep his commandments and his statutes which are written in this book of the law, if you turn to Yahweh your God with all your heart and with all your soul.

2Cor 12:11 **I have become foolish** in boasting. You compelled me, for **I ought to have been commended by you**, for I am **in no way inferior to the very best apostles, though I am nothing**. **12** The signs of an **apostle** were performed among you in all perseverance, in **signs** and **wonders** and **mighty works**.

NOTE: The final three echoes in 2 Corinthians 12:12, *signs*, *wonders* and *mighty works* are witnesses of God's having sent Paul as his apostle. Their echoes are the three witnesses of God's restoration of his people: that when it comes to those opposing that restoration that God will personally and directly put his curses on "your enemies," "those who hate you," and those who "persecuted you." God's desire, of course, is not that the curses will bring destruction, but rather that they will lead those persons and nations to reconsider their ways and turn to God in repentance. In both Deuteronomy and 2 Corinthians we see repentance as the ultimate goal, both within the people of God, and outside of it, so that they may be brought into the covenants of promise (Eph. 2:12).

De 30:11 For this commandment which I command you today is not too hard for you or too far off. **12** It is not in heaven, that you should say, "Who will go up for us to heaven, bring it to us, and let us hear it, that we may do it?" **13** Neither is it beyond the sea, that you should say, "**Who will go over the sea for us, bring it to us**, and let us hear it, that we may do it?" **14** But **the word is very near to you**, in your mouth and in your heart, that you may do it.

12Cor 2:13 For what is there in which you were made inferior **to the rest of the assemblies**, unless it is that **I myself was not a burden to you**? Forgive me this wrong!

NOTE: A temptation existed within Israel to consider that they had been disadvantaged by God as compared to other nations, for having received a difficult commandment. Moses got ahead of this tendency and addressed it. Paul in turn addresses in advance his expectation that by criticizing the Corinthians he was being harder on them than the rest of the assemblies.

De 30:15 Behold, I have set before you today life and prosperity, and death and evil, **16** in that I command you today to **love** Yahweh your God, to walk in his ways, and to keep his commandments, his statutes, and his ordinances, that you may live and multiply, and that Yahweh your God may bless you in the land where you go in to possess it. **17** But if your heart turns away, and you will not hear, but are drawn away and worship other gods, and serve them, **18** I declare to you today that you will surely perish. You will not prolong your days in the land where you pass over the Jordan to go in to possess it. **19** I call heaven and earth to witness against you today, that I have set before you life and death, the blessing and the curse. Therefore choose life, that you may live, **you and your descendants**, **20** to **love** Yahweh your God, to obey his voice, and to cling to him; for he is your life, and the length of your days, that you may dwell in the land which Yahweh swore to your fathers, to Abraham, to Isaac, and to Jacob, to give them.

2Cor 12:14 Behold, this is the third time I am ready to come to you, and I will not be a burden to you; for I seek not your possessions, but you. For the children ought not to save up for the parents, but the **parents for the children**. 15 I will most gladly spend and be spent for your souls. If I **love** you more, am I to be **loved** less?

NOTE: [Nitzavim ends.] This sectional pairing, is not as orderly as most. We have to look deeper to see what Paul was echoing. Notice for instance, that the word "love" is used exactly twice in both sides of this pairing. Paul's "parents for the children" clearly echoes "you and your descendants."

NOTE: Paul's use of "third time" is quite confusing at first glance. He follows that with three declaratives: "I am ready to come," "I will not be a burden," and "I seek not your possessions." The Deuteronomy side of this pairing has three strong declaratives using the word "life" in Deut. 30:19-20. Paul said what he seeks is "them," which echoes beautifully God's heart for his people to simply have "life," not that God would use their obedience as an excuse to control them.

Deuteronomy 31   2 Cor. 12:16

De 31:1 Moses went and spoke these words to all Israel. **2** He said to them, I am one hundred twenty years old today. I can no more go out and come in. **Yahweh has said to me, You shall not go over this Jordan**. **3** Yahweh your God himself will go over before you. He will destroy these nations from before you, and you shall dispossess them. Joshua will go over before you, as Yahweh has spoken. **4** Yahweh will do to them as he did to Sihon and to Og, the kings of the Amorites, and to their land, when he destroyed them. **5** Yahweh will deliver them up before you, and you shall do to them according to all the commandment which I have commanded you. **6** Be strong and courageous. Don't be afraid or scared of them, for Yahweh your God himself is who goes with you. He will not fail you nor forsake you.

2Cor 12:16 But be it so, I didn't myself burden you. But, **being crafty, I caught you with deception**.

NOTE: [Vayelech.] For almost the entire time in the wilderness, the children of Israel had expected that Moses would personally lead them into the promised land. But early in Deuteronomy 1:37 he informs them that God was not going to let him enter, but that it would simply be his words -- Gods commandments -- that they must carry into the Promised Land, not his physical presence. Similarly Paul states that he was not going to burden them with a personal visit, even though he had threatened to visit.

De 31:7 Moses called to Joshua and said to him in the sight of all Israel, Be strong and courageous, for you shall go with this people into the land which Yahweh has sworn to their fathers to give them; and you shall cause them to inherit it. **8 Yahweh himself is who goes before you. He will be with you**. He will not fail you nor forsake you. Don't be afraid, and don't be dismayed.

2Cor 12:17 Did I take advantage of you by anyone of those whom I have sent to you?

18 I exhorted Titus, and I sent the brother with him. Did Titus take any advantage of you? **Didn't we walk in the same spirit? Didn't we walk in the same steps?**

NOTE: Just as Moses called Joshua and said to him "you shall go," Paul had decided to send Titus to visit the church in Corinth. And just as Moses reframes the people's perception of Joshua as being who will walk under the leadership of Yahweh himself, so Paul reframes the church's perception of Titus as a man who, like Paul, was walking in the spirit as Paul, and in the same steps as Paul. The use of the word "steps" loudly echoes Joshua's call to enter the Promised Land.

De 31:9 Moses wrote this law and delivered it **to the priests the sons of Levi**, who carried the ark of Yahweh's covenant, and to all the elders of Israel. **10** Moses commanded them, saying, At the end of every seven years, in the set time of the year of release, **in the feast of booths**, **11** when all Israel has come to appear before Yahweh your God in the place which he will choose, you shall read this law before all Israel in their hearing. **12 Assemble the people, the men and the women and the little ones, and the foreigners who are within your gates, that they may hear, learn, fear Yahweh your God,** and observe to do **all the words of this law**, **13** and that their children, who have not known, may hear and learn to fear Yahweh your God, as long as you live in the land **where you go over the Jordan to possess it**.

2Cor 12:19 Again, do you think that **we are excusing ourselves** to you? **In the sight of God** we **speak in Christ**. But **all things**, beloved, are **for your edifying**.

NOTE: The Levities were not exempt from the same command given to all the people. In the feast of Booths, the people were to sleep in temporary shelters as a reminder that they were under the sight of God. The word "edifying" in 2 Corinthians 12:19 literally means upbuilding, which echoes the active "possessing" of the land by the children of Israel.

De 31:14 Yahweh said to Moses, Behold, your days approach that you must die. Call Joshua, and present yourselves in the Tent of Meeting, that I may commission him. Moses and Joshua went, and presented themselves in the Tent of Meeting. **15** Yahweh appeared in the Tent in a pillar of cloud, and the pillar of cloud stood over the door of the Tent. **16** Yahweh said to Moses, Behold, you shall sleep with your fathers. This people will rise up and play the prostitute after the strange gods of the land where they go to be among them, and will forsake me and break my covenant which I have made with them. **17** Then my anger shall be kindled against them in that day, and I will forsake them, and I will hide my face from them, and they shall be devoured, and many evils and troubles shall come on them; so that they will say in that day, "Haven't these evils come on us because our God is not among us?" **18** I will surely hide my face in that day for all the evil which they have done, in that they have turned to other gods.

De 19 Now therefore write this song for yourselves, and teach it to the children of Israel. Put it in their mouths, that this song may be a **witness for me against the children of Israel**. **20** For when I have brought them into the land which I swore to their fathers, flowing with milk and honey, and they have eaten and filled themselves, and grown fat, then they will turn to other gods, and serve them, and despise me, and break my covenant. **21** It will happen, when many evils and troubles have come on them, **that this song will testify before them as a witness; for it will not be forgotten out of the mouths of their offspring**; for I know their ways and what they are doing today, before I have brought them into the land which I promised them. **22** So Moses wrote this song the same day, and taught it to the children of Israel.

2Cor 12:20 For I am afraid that perhaps when I come, **I might find you not the way I want to**,

and that **I might be found by you as you don't desire**, that perhaps there would be

strife, jealousy, outbursts of anger, factions, slander, whisperings, proud thoughts, or riots,

NOTE: The first 2 Corinthians 12:20 phrase "I might find you not the way I want to" echoes "witness for me against the children of Israel." Next, Moses's song contained elements that no people would want to hear spoken over them, echoing Paul's comment "I might be found by you as you don't desire." The eight sins in 2 Corinthians beginning with *strife* and ending with *riots*, may possibly echo the eight prophesied sins in Deuteronomy beginning with in Deuteronomy 31:16 *rise up*, and ending in Deut. 31:20, with the second instance of *break my covenant.*

De 31:23 He commissioned Joshua the son of Nun, and said, Be strong and courageous; for you shall bring the children of Israel into the land which I swore to them. I will be with you.

24 When Moses had finished writing the words of this law in a book, until they were finished, **25** Moses commanded the Levites, who carried the ark of Yahweh's covenant, saying, **26** Take this book of the law, and put it by the side of the ark of Yahweh your God's covenant, that it may be there for a witness against you. **27** For I know your rebellion and your stiff neck. Behold, while I am yet alive with you today, you have been rebellious against Yahweh. How much more after my death? **28** Assemble to **me** all the elders of your tribes and your officers, that I may speak these words in their ears, and call heaven and earth to witness against them. **29** For I know that after my death **you** will utterly corrupt yourselves, and turn away from the way which I have commanded you; and evil will happen to you in the latter days, because you will do that which is evil in Yahweh's sight, to provoke him to anger through the work of your hands.

30 Moses spoke in the ears of all the assembly of Israel the words of this song, until they were finished.

2**Cor 12:21** lest, when I come again, my God would humble **me** before **you**, and I would **mourn for many of those who have sinned before now**, and not repented of the uncleanness, sexual immorality, and lustfulness which they committed.

NOTE: [Vayelech ends.] Moses's song includes elements of mourning by Moses over the people's sin. Nevertheless Moses's song is meant as a call for repentance, not just mourning. In the same way, Paul further explains that his mourning would be for those who have not yet repented.

Deuteronomy 32

De 32:1 Give ear, you heavens, and I will speak.

Let the earth hear the words of my mouth.

2 My doctrine will drop as the rain. My speech will condense as the dew, as the small rain on the tender grass, as the showers on the herb.

3 For I will proclaim Yahweh's name. Ascribe greatness to our God!

4 The Rock: his work is perfect, for all his ways are just. A God of faithfulness who does no wrong, just and right is he.

NOTE: [Haazinu.] Paul seems to skip past these beginning verses of the song that comprises most of Deuteronomy 32.

De 32:5 They have dealt corruptly with him. They are not his children, because of their defect. **They are a perverse and crooked generation**.

6 Is this the way you repay Yahweh, foolish and unwise people? Isn't he your father who has bought you? He has made you and established you.

7 Remember the days of old. Consider the years of many generations. Ask your father, and he will show you; your elders, and they will tell you.

8 When the Most High gave to the nations their inheritance, when he separated the children of men, he set the bounds of the peoples according to the number of the children of Israel.

9 For Yahweh's portion is his people. Jacob is the lot of his inheritance.

10 He found him in a desert land, in the waste howling wilderness. He surrounded him. He cared for him. He kept him as the apple of his eye.

11 As an eagle that stirs up her nest, that flutters over her young, he spread abroad his wings, he took them, he bore them on his pinions.

12 Yahweh alone led him. There was no foreign god with him.

13 He made him ride on the high places of the earth. He ate the increase of the field. He caused him to suck honey out of the rock, oil out of the flinty rock;

14 butter of the herd, and milk of the flock, with fat of lambs, rams of the breed of Bashan, and goats, with the finest of the wheat. Of the blood of the grape, you drank wine.

15 But Jeshurun grew fat, and kicked. You have grown fat. You have grown thick. You have become sleek. Then he abandoned God who made him, and rejected the Rock of his salvation.

16 They moved him to jealousy with strange gods. They provoked him to anger with **abominations**.

17 They **sacrificed to demons**, not God, to gods that they didn't know, to **new gods that came up** recently, which your fathers **didn't dread**.

2Cor 12:21 lest, when I come again, my God would humble me before you, and I would mourn for many of those who have **sinned before now**, and not repented of the **uncleanness**, **sexual immorality**, and **lustfulness** which they **committed**.

NOTE: The phrase "sacrificed to demons" echoes "sexual immorality" (Greek: *porneia*) due to the sexual acts that accompany those sacrifices. The word "dread" (Heb. *Saar*) means "to be acquainted with" echoes committed (Greek: *prasso*) which can also be translated as practiced, attended, or collected. In other words, they committed those sins rather than dreading them.

De 32:18 Of the Rock who became your father, you are unmindful, and have forgotten God who gave you birth.

19 Yahweh saw and abhorred, because of the provocation of his sons and his daughters.

20 He said, "I will hide my face from them. I will see what their end will be; for they are a very perverse generation, children in whom is no faithfulness.

21 They have moved me to jealousy with that which is not God. They have provoked me to anger with their vanities. I will move them to jealousy with those who are not a people. I will provoke them to anger with a foolish nation.

22 For a fire is kindled in my anger, that burns to the lowest Sheol, devours the earth with its increase, and sets the foundations of the mountains on fire.

23 I will heap evils on them. I will spend my arrows on them.

24 They shall be wasted with hunger, and devoured with burning heat and bitter destruction. I will send the teeth of animals on them, with the venom of crawling things of the dust.

25 Outside, the sword will bereave, and in the rooms, terror on both young man and virgin, the nursing infant with the gray-haired man.

26 I said that I would scatter them afar. I would make their memory to cease from among men;

27 were it not that I feared the provocation of the enemy, lest their adversaries should judge wrongly, lest they should say, "Our hand is exalted, Yahweh has not done all this."

28 For they are a nation void of counsel. There is no understanding in them.

29 Oh that they were wise, that they understood this, that they would consider their latter end!

30 How could one chase a thousand, and two put ten thousand to flight, unless their Rock had sold them, and Yahweh had delivered them up?

NOTE: Paul seems to skip past these verses of the song.

De 32:30 How could one chase a thousand, and two put ten thousand to flight, unless their Rock had sold them, and Yahweh had delivered them up?

31 For their rock is not as our Rock, even our enemies themselves concede.

32 For their vine is of the vine of Sodom, of the fields of Gomorrah. Their grapes are grapes of gall. Their clusters are bitter.

33 Their wine is the poison of serpents, the cruel venom of asps.

34 Isn't this laid up in store with me, sealed up among my treasures?

35 Vengeance is mine, and recompense, at the time when their foot slides; for the day of their calamity is at hand. Their doom rushes at them.

36 For Yahweh will judge his people, and have compassion on his servants, when he sees that their power is gone, that there is no one remaining, shut up or left at large.

37 He will say, "Where are their gods, the rock in which they took refuge;

38 which ate the fat of their sacrifices, and drank the wine of their drink offering? Let them rise up and help you! Let them be your protection.

39 See now that I myself am he. There is no god with me. I kill and I make alive. I wound and I heal. There is no one who can deliver out of my hand.

40 For I lift up my hand to heaven and say, As I live forever,

41 if I sharpen my glittering sword, my hand grasps it in judgment; I will take vengeance on my adversaries, and will repay those who hate me.

42 I will make my arrows drunk with blood. My sword shall devour flesh with the blood of the slain and the captives, from the head of the leaders of the enemy.

43 Rejoice, you nations, with his people, for he will avenge the blood of his servants. He will take vengeance on his adversaries, and will make atonement for his land and for his people."

NOTE: Paul seems to skip past these final verses of the song.

Deuteronomy 32:44	2 Cor. 13

De 32:44 Moses came and spoke all the words of this **song** in the ears of the people, he and Joshua the son of Nun. **45** When Moses had finished <u>speaking all these words</u> to all Israel, **46** he said to them, Set your heart to all the words which I *testify* to you today, which you shall command your children to observe to do, all the <u>words</u> of this law. **47** For it is no vain thing for you, because it is your life, and through this thing you shall prolong your days in the land, where you go over the Jordan to possess it.

2Cor 13:1 This is the **third time** I am coming to you. "At the <u>**mouth**</u> of *two or three witnesses* shall every <u>word</u> be established."

NOTE: Regarding the first echo, "song" echoing "third time," the reasoning is as follows. After God gives instructions to Moses about the need to sing a song -- the word "song" used three times by God in Deuteronomy 31:19, 19 and 21 -- Moses obeys. The verses detailing his obedience also use the word "song" three times in Deut. 31:22, 30 and 32:44.

NOTE: Regarding the third echo, "two or three witnesses" is also echoed in Deuteronomy as follows. The song is stated to have been sung by both Moses and Joshua (Deut. 32:44), and the third witness is God himself (Deut. 31:19).

De 32:48 Yahweh spoke to Moses that same day, saying, **49** "Go up into this mountain of Abarim, to Mount Nebo, which is in the land of Moab, that is opposite Jericho; and see the land of Canaan, which I give to the children of Israel for a possession. **50** Die on the mountain where you go up, and be gathered to your people, as Aaron your brother died on Mount Hor, and was gathered to his people; **51** because you trespassed against me among the children of Israel at the waters of Meribah of Kadesh, in the wilderness of Zin; because **you didn't uphold my holiness among the children of Israel**. **52** For you shall <u>see the land from a distance</u>; but *you shall not go there* into the <u>land which I give the children of Israel</u>.

2Cor 13:2 I have warned previously, and I warn again, as when I was present the second time, so now, being absent, I write to those who have sinned before now and to all the rest that **if I come again, I will not spare**; **3** seeing that you <u>**seek a proof of Christ who speaks in me**</u> who is not weak, but is powerful in you. **4** For he was crucified through weakness, yet he lives through the power of God. *For we also are weak in him, but we will live with him* through the <u>power of God toward you</u>.

NOTE: [Haazinu ends.]

Deuteronomy 33   2 Cor. 13:5

De 33:1 This is the blessing with which Moses the man of God blessed the children of Israel before his death. **2** He said, "Yahweh came from Sinai, and rose from Seir to them. He shone from Mount Paran. He came from the ten thousands of holy ones. At his right hand was a fiery law for them.

3 Yes, he loves the people. **All his saints are in your hand. They sat down at your feet. Each receives your words**. **4** Moses commanded us a law, an inheritance for the assembly of Jacob. **5 He was king in Jeshurun**, when the heads of the people were gathered, all the tribes of Israel together. **6** Let Reuben live, and not die; **Nor let his men be few**."

2Cor 13:5 **Examine yourselves, whether you are in the faith**. Test your own selves. Or **don't you know about your own selves, that Jesus Christ is in you**?— unless indeed you are disqualified. **6** But I hope that you will **know that we aren't disqualified**.

NOTE: [V'Zot HaBerachah.] Jeshurun is a name for Israel, therefore "He was *king in* Jeshurun echoes "don't you know…that Jesus Christ is *in you*?"

De 33:7 This is for Judah. He said, "Hear, Yahweh, the voice of Judah. Bring him in to his people. With his hands **he contended** for himself. You shall be a help against his adversaries."

8 About Levi he said, "Your Thummim and your Urim are with your godly one, whom you **proved** at Massah, with whom you contended at the waters of Meribah. **9** He said of his father, and of his mother, 'I have not seen him.' He didn't acknowledge his brothers, nor did he know his own children; **for they have observed your word**, and **keep your covenant**. **10** They shall teach Jacob your ordinances, and Israel your law. They shall put incense before you, and whole burnt offering on your altar. **11** Yahweh, bless his skills. Accept the work of his hands. Strike through the hips of those who rise up against him, of those who hate him, that they not rise again."

12 About Benjamin he said, "The beloved of Yahweh will dwell in safety by him. He covers him all day long. He dwells between his shoulders."

2**Cor 13:7** Now

I pray to God that you do no evil; not that we may appear **approved**, but that you may **do that which is honorable**, though we may **seem to have failed**.

De 33:13 About Joseph he said, "His land is blessed by Yahweh, for the precious things of the heavens, for the dew, for the deep that couches beneath, **14** for the precious things of the fruits of the sun, for the precious things that the moon can yield, **15** for the best things of the ancient mountains, for the precious things of the everlasting hills, **16** for the precious things of the earth and its fullness, **the good will of him who lived in the bush**. Let this come on the head of Joseph, on the crown of the head of him who was separated from his brothers. **17** **Majesty belongs to the firstborn of his herd. His horns are the horns of the wild ox**. With them he will push all the peoples to the ends of the earth. They are the ten thousands of Ephraim. They are the thousands of Manasseh."

18 About Zebulun he said, "Rejoice, Zebulun, in your going out; and Issachar, in your tents. **19** They will call the peoples to the mountain. There they will offer sacrifices of righteousness, for they will draw out the abundance of the seas, the hidden treasures of the sand."

20 About Gad he said, "He who enlarges Gad is blessed. He dwells as a lioness, and tears the arm, yes, the crown of the head. **21** He provided the first part for himself, for the lawgiver's portion was reserved for him. He came with the heads of the people. He executed the righteousness of Yahweh, His ordinances with Israel."

22 About Dan he said, "Dan is a lion's cub that leaps out of Bashan."

23 About Naphtali he said, "Naphtali, satisfied with favor, full of Yahweh's blessing, possess the west and the south."

24 About Asher he said, "Asher is blessed with children. Let him be acceptable to his brothers. Let him dip his foot in oil. **25** Your bars will be iron and bronze. As your days, so your strength will be.

2Cor 13:8 For **we can do nothing against the truth, but for the truth**. 9 For we rejoice when <u>we are weak and you are strong</u>. We also pray for this: <u>your becoming perfect</u>.

NOTE: <u>The tribe of Simeon is notably absent</u> from the blessings. This echoes Paul's words "your becoming perfect" which can also be translated "your becoming complete." The second census at the end of the forty years shows the count of persons from the tribe of Simeon to be much reduced from count of the first census.

NOTE: In Deuteronomy 33:16, the phrase "the good will of him who lived in the bush" is widely believed to be referring to Moses's encounter with God in the burning bush. The first thing Moses learned in that encounter was the "truth" of the ground he was standing upon. Had he not removed the sandals from his feet, it would not have altered the truth of the moment, echoing "we can do nothing against the truth," yet this removal can be seen as the first step Moses took "for the truth" in revealing to the nation of Israel God's *good will* to bring that nation out of slavery.

De 33:26 There is no one like **God, Jeshurun**, who rides on the heavens for your help, in his **excellency on the skies. 27 The eternal God is your dwelling place**. Underneath are the everlasting arms. He thrust out the enemy from before you, and said, 'Destroy!' **28** Israel dwells in safety, the fountain of Jacob alone, in a land of grain and new wine. Yes, his heavens drop **down** dew. **29** You are happy, Israel! Who is like you, a people saved by Yahweh, the shield of your help, the sword of your excellency? Your enemies will submit themselves to you. You will tread on their high places.

2Cor 13:10 For this cause I write these things while absent, that I may not deal sharply when present, according to the authority which the **Lord** gave me for **building up** and not for tearing **down**.

Deuteronomy 34

2 Cor. 13:11

De 34:1 **Moses went up from the plains of Moab to Mount Nebo, to the top of Pisgah, that is opposite Jericho**. **Yahweh showed him all the land** of <u>Gilead</u> to <u>Dan</u>, **2** and all <u>Naphtali</u>, and the land of <u>Ephraim</u> and <u>Manasseh</u>, and all the land of <u>Judah</u>, to the <u>Western Sea</u>, **3** and the <u>South</u>, and the <u>Plain of the valley of Jericho the city of palm trees</u>, to <u>Zoar</u>. **4** Yahweh said to him, "This is the land which I swore to Abraham, to Isaac, and to Jacob, saying, 'I will give it to your offspring.' I have caused you to see it with your eyes, but you shall not go over there." **5** So Moses the servant of Yahweh died there in the land of Moab, according to Yahweh's word. **6** He buried him in the valley in the land of Moab opposite Beth Peor, but no man knows where his tomb is to this day. **7** Moses was one hundred twenty years old when he died. His eye was not dim, nor his strength gone.

2Cor 13:11a
<u>Finally, brothers</u>,

rejoice!

<u>Be perfected. Be comforted.</u>

NOTE: Deuteronomy 34:1 begins the final chapter of Deuteronomy, and tells of the end of Moses's life on earth. The phrase "Yahweh showed him all the land" would have been a moment of great rejoicing for Moses, echoing the word "rejoice" (echo 2). The phrase "be comforted" echoing the 10 portions of the land, recalls a similar pattern in 2 Corinthians Ch. 1, where 10 uses of "comfort" echo the 10 portions of the land (Deut. 1:6). But this time Paul adds "be perfected" (or complete) as well.

De 34:4 Yahweh said to him, "This is the land which I swore to Abraham, to Isaac, and to Jacob, saying, 'I will give it to your offspring.' I have caused you to see it with your eyes, but you shall not go over there." 5 So Moses the servant of Yahweh died there in the land of Moab, according to Yahweh's word. **6** He buried him in the valley in the land of Moab opposite Beth Peor, but no man knows where his tomb is to this day. **7** Moses was one hundred twenty years old when he died. His eye was not dim, nor his strength gone.

2Cor 13:11b **Be of the same mind.** Live in peace, and the God of love and peace will be with you.

NOTE: Moses steps into agreement with God and his forefathers about God's great purposes (echo 1). Next, Moses no longer contends with Yahweh about his decisions (echo 2). Then God gave himself to Moses, burying him, never leaving Moses alone for even a second (echo 3).

De 34:8 The children of Israel wept for Moses in the plains of Moab thirty days, until the days of weeping in the mourning for Moses were ended.

2Cor 13:12 **Greet one another with a holy kiss.** 13 All the saints greet you.

NOTE: In the first echo, the children of Israel wept, meaning that tears came down their cheeks. The holy kiss was presumably on the cheek, and may well be something that is especially appropriate to give in a time of mourning. In the second echo, the days of weeping and mourning for Moses ended. Paul's echo here seems unexpected. One possible explanation is that Paul believes that "all the saints" refers not only to those living in other places on earth, but those who have passed on as well. Indeed, Abraham, Isaac and Jacob are mentioned in Deuteronomy 34:4, just four verses earlier, and additionally Jesus declares that those three persons are not dead, but living (Matthew 22:32).

De 34:9 Joshua the son of Nun was full of the spirit of wisdom, for Moses had laid his hands on him. The children of Israel listened to him, and did as Yahweh commanded Moses. 10 Since then, no prophet has risen in Israel like Moses, whom Yahweh knew face to face, 11 in all the signs and the wonders which Yahweh sent him to do in the land of Egypt, to Pharaoh, and to all his servants, and to all his land,	2Cor 13:14a The **grace of the Lord Jesus Christ**, God's love,

NOTE: In the first echo, Joshua is both a type of Christ, as well as a type of us who receive the grace of our Lord Jesus through the impartation of the spirit, once Jesus ascended to heaven. In the second echo, these astounding words being spoken by God about Moses show God's tremendous love for Moses. Notice that if one looks at both sides of the second echo, a hidden reference to John 3:16 is present: God so LOVED the world that he SENT his only son…" This dual concept of Moses and Jesus being paired together in scripture finds it scriptural support in the *song of Moses and the Lamb* (Revelation 15:3).

De 34:12 and in all the mighty hand, and in all the awesome deeds, which Moses did **in the sight of all Israel**.	2Cor 13:14b and **the fellowship of the Holy Spirit be with you all**. Amen.

NOTE: [V'Zot HaBerachah ends.] The work of the Exodus from Egypt was previously echoed by Paul as also being connected to God's Spirit in (2 Corinthians 3:17). Concluding both books, the last echo connects *all Israel* with *all Corinthians*, but perhaps more generally, all who read Paul's letter. That certainly includes the all the readers who have now reached the conclusion of this, Volume V, of the Echoes Bible. Amen.

THE STORY OF THE ECHOES BIBLE

The discovery of the ancient connections between Paul's New Testament letters and the Old Testament books was made by John David Pitcher in 2008. He has published material on these connections under the title *The Oldest Midrash*. His discoveries were made primarily through linguistic analysis of the Septuagint in comparison with the New Testament. For more information see echoesbible.org/john-david-pitcher/.

When Bob O'Dell first learned of David's discoveries, he began to examine them carefully to determine whether the claims were true. David asserted in 2015 that six of Paul's epistles connected to major books of the Old Testament: Genesis to Hebrews, Exodus to Galatians, Leviticus to Romans, Numbers to 2 Timothy, Deuteronomy to 1 Timothy, and Joshua to Titus—discoveries made between 2008 and 2012. Once learning of the discovery, Bob devoted nine months to studying David's assertions in the first three pairings listed above, declaring David's discoveries to be valid. Bob found that, although he already considered himself skilled in "seeing Jesus in every page of the Old Testament," it nevertheless required time to begin perceiving those passages in the same light in which Paul himself had seen them. Paul saw far more, and Bob had to learn how Paul approached those texts—an approach that was both deeper and, at times, more obvious than he expected. It was as though, after many years of Bible study, Bob was reading the Scriptures again for the first time. Yet it was not that the truth itself was new, for Paul's words had not changed. Rather, the primary insight lay in the beauty and awe of how Paul conceptualized the Old Testament texts within the life of ancient Israel. The work of Christ was fully prefigured! It is no wonder that Paul would declare that all Scripture is useful for doctrine.

Over the next five years, with new eyes to perceive Paul's writings, Bob O'Dell combined linguistic analysis with thematic resonance, thereby both deepening the connections identified in David's discoveries and making additional, as yet unpublished discoveries as well. Whereas David has focused on the midrashic aspect of Paul's literary decisions within the academic realm, Bob has concentrated on the echoes between the Testaments— showing how each text further contextualizes and illuminates the other. His desire was that serious Bible students around the world might experience what he himself experienced: to be filled with awe and wonder at God, His Word, and the finished work of His Son. This has led to the formation of the Echoes Bible Foundation, a U.S. based 501(c)3 organization whose mission is to disseminate these insights both in print and online. Bob and David remain close friends.

The World English Bible (WEB) is used for the text due to its non-copyright status. The Echoes Bible Foundation considers the decision by eBible.org to publish a non-copyrighted modern English version of the Bible based on the non-copyrighted *New American Standard 1901*, to be a magnificent gift to the modern world.

For more on the Echoes Bible see echoesbible.org or echoesbible.com.

www.ingramcontent.com/pod-product-compliance
Lightning Source LLC
Chambersburg PA
CBHW070049040426
42331CB00034B/2652